DAUGHTERS OF THE CANTON DELTA

Daughters of the Canton Delta

*Marriage Patterns and
Economic Strategies in South China,
1860-1930*

Janice E. Stockard

STANFORD UNIVERSITY PRESS
Stanford, California

Stanford University Press
Stanford, California
© 1989 by the Board of Trustees of the
Leland Stanford Junior University
Printed in the United States of America

Original printing 1989
Last figure below indicates year of this printing:
01   00   99   98   97   96   95   94   93   92

Published with the assistance of a
special grant from the Stanford
University Faculty Publication
Fund to help support nonfaculty
work originating at Stanford.

CIP data appear at the end of the book

Maps and calligraphy by Zumou Yue

To my mother
Elizabeth Welch Stockard

and to the memory of my father
Caswell Miles Stockard, Jr.

Preface

In the spring of 1979, I arrived in Hong Kong to begin my field-work in anthropology. Over the course of the next two-and-one-half years, what began as a project focused on contemporary marriage and labor patterns in urban Hong Kong became instead a project about historical patterns in the Canton Delta countryside. Well into the first year of my research, I learned—quite by accident during one fortuitous interview—of an unorthodox marriage pattern that had prevailed in the Canton Delta in traditional times. Interviewing was never again quite the same. Inspired by a sense of discovery, my research assistant and I set forth to interview elderly women from villages over a widespread area in the Delta. I hoped to reconstruct from our informants' accounts a marriage system that had historically been subject to misinterpretation (because of the cultural bias of outsiders) and to political repression. (It is, of course, with some irony that I speak of "discovering" the way millions of people had been marrying for generations.) This book describes the unorthodox marriage system of the Canton Delta and analyzes the changes it underwent during one historical period.

Many people made this project possible. I am grateful to my professors in the Department of Anthropology at Stanford University, my advisor, Arthur P. Wolf, G. William Skinner, and Jane F. Collier, for their continued support and for providing me with the ethnographic and analytic skills that enabled me to conduct this research. I also wish to acknowledge the inspired and tireless efforts of the late Hei-tak Wu in preparing me to speak and think in Cantonese. In Hong Kong, I was given the full use of the facilities of the Centre of Asian Studies at the University of Hong Kong, and I am especially grateful to Edward K. Y. Chen and Conoor Kripalani-Thadani of the Centre for their support. None of my interviews would have been possible without James Hayes, whose reputation in Hong Kong opened doors for me at the many retirement homes, temporary housing shelters for the elderly, and vegetarian halls that were the homes of my informants. I benefited much from his enthusiasm for my research and his expertise in local Chinese culture and history. I owe a very special debt of gratitude to my good friend and research assistant, Eunice Mei-wan Ku, who shared with me both the early frustrations and later rewards of the fieldwork experience. Over the years of research, Eunice proved to be the ablest of field-workers, and I like to think that together we made a particularly effective research team. There are many who made my work in Hong Kong possible through their friendship and hospitality. I especially thank Robert and Susan Ribeiro, Frank and Catherine King, Pavala Velu, Peter Wesley-Smith, Jonathan Grant, John and Susan Anderson, and Rusty and Sarah Todd for providing me with a home away from home. Funding for this project was provided in part by the Institute for Research on Women and Gender and the Center for Research in International Studies at Stanford.

Since the completion of my doctoral dissertation in 1985, the Center for Chinese Studies at the University of California, Berkeley, has opened its facilities for my research and writing, as well as supported further fieldwork in Hong Kong. I especially thank

Joyce Kallgren of the Center for her support during this period. As a recipient of a Mellon postdoctoral fellowship from the American Council of Learned Societies in 1985–86, I was able to pursue further field and archival research. A special tour of the Canton Delta in 1986 was made possible through the efforts of officials of the Sundak (Shun-te) County Association in Hong Kong and of Sundak county in China. I thank the latter for giving me the opportunity to see many of the villages and towns that my informants call home and for showing me the historical technology of the local silk-reeling industry, which played an important role in the lives of many of my informants.

I owe a special debt of gratitude to my editor at Stanford Press, Muriel Bell, who contributed so much to the development of this book. Beyond her editorial expertise and enthusiasm for the research, her encouragement of its author contributed much to the shape of the final book. I also thank John Ziemer of Stanford Press for his insightful comments on the manuscript, which benefited from his knowledge in the China field. The drawings of the Canton Delta countryside that illustrate this book were located by Joseph S. P. Ting, Assistant Curator of the Hong Kong Art Museum, to whom I am most grateful. And for their stimulating comments on various drafts of this manuscript, I thank Jane F. Collier, David Faure, John Shepherd, Helen Siu, G. William Skinner, and Arthur P. Wolf, as well as Zumou Yue, who also skillfully and beautifully executed the maps that appear in this book.

Thanks are also due members of my family, including Elizabeth Stockard, Nathan Stockard, Sally and Frank Ashton, and Clark Stockard, for their support and encouragement through the years of fieldwork and writing.

I also wish to acknowledge Marjorie Topley for her pioneering work on marriage practices in the Canton Delta, which opened up this subject for research. And, finally, to the many women from the Canton Delta who were my informants, I owe a special debt of gratitude, for it is their life stories that are the heart of this book.

J. E. S.

Contents

Maps

Six pages of photographs follow page 78.

Note on Romanization

The marriage system described in this book has often been distorted in the literature, in part because it has been misperceived by both Westerners and Chinese from outside the Canton Delta. Since language itself has proved to be one source of distortion—something seems to get lost in the translation from Cantonese (the regional dialect) to Mandarin (the "national" dialect)—I have decided to provide the reader with the original Cantonese terms and expressions. These are romanized according to the Yale system of Cantonese romanization, except where otherwise noted in Appendix B. Cantonese place-names are also romanized according to the Yale system except for the city of Canton. (See Appendix C for Chinese characters for these places.) For information on the Yale system, see Huang 1970.

DAUGHTERS OF THE CANTON DELTA

1

Delayed Transfer Marriage

From the Canton Delta of the early twentieth century came reports of a startling phenomenon: wives who refused to live with their husbands and young women who refused to marry at all. In traditional Chinese society—a society shaped and constrained by strongly patriarchal Confucian values—what could explain this unorthodox behavior?

In traditional Chinese society marriage was virtually universal for women. Girls were married off shortly after puberty in "blind" marriages arranged by senior family members. The transition from daughter to wife was not easy. Anthropologists and other observers have described the traumatic experience of the new bride, torn from her family and installed, dependent and powerless, in her husband's family home.* Cut off from her natal family, the young wife struggled to establish herself in her husband's family. There, under the strict supervision of her mother-

*See especially M. Wolf 1972.

in-law, she was expected to perform the duties of household drudge. As in other patrilineal societies, a primary goal for the young wife was to bear sons, thereby providing for the continuation of her husband's family and the male descent line. By doing so, a wife established herself more firmly within her husband's family, and later, through the manipulation of her adult sons, she realized some measure of power in a society that denied her formal authority. Thus, over the course of her life cycle, with adult sons and daughters-in-law to serve and support her, a wife realized some improvement in her lot. Although drawn with broad strokes, this sketch conveys the basic outlines of the orthodox or "major" marriage pattern that characterized traditional Chinese society virtually everywhere in China.* Marriage according to the major pattern entailed both the immediate transfer of the bride to her husband's family home and her immediate assumption there of obligations, including domestic labor, childbearing, and child rearing.

Before the establishment of the People's Republic of China in 1949, major marriage was the cultural-ideal form of marriage, celebrated in Confucian ideology and the focus of a marriage system that also included other, less prestigious forms of marriage. Perhaps the most widely practiced of the alternatives to major marriage was uxorilocal marriage, in which the husband settled at marriage in the wife's family home. Uxorilocal marriages were negotiated under the duress of circumstances, specifically the absence of sons, unfavorable to the attainment of major marriage. Another alternative to major marriage, less widely distributed than uxorilocal marriage, was minor marriage, in which young girls were acquired by families who raised them as future wives for their sons. Arthur Wolf has shown that in certain counties in Fukien, Taiwan, and northern Kwangtung, minor marriages accounted for the majority of first marriages (A. Wolf and Huang 1980). However, like uxorilocal marriage, minor marriage was acknowledged to be an inferior form of mar-

---

*Arthur Wolf coined the term "major marriage" to describe the orthodox model of marriage in traditional Chinese society. See A. Wolf and Huang 1980.

riage, a remedy to circumstances unfavorable to major marriage. In short, major marriage defined a marriage system that encompassed virtually all of traditional Chinese society, with alternative forms of marriage—including uxorilocal and minor marriage—forming inferior marriage options, occurring with varying frequencies in different regions.

In the discussion that follows, I describe yet another form of marriage in traditional Chinese society—a form I call "delayed transfer marriage"—and relate how it was practiced within a specific area in the Canton Delta of Kwangtung province. Although delayed transfer marriage has not previously been described in the ethnographic literature on the Canton Delta, its imprint is apparent in the special forms of "marriage resistance" reported by Marjorie Topley (1975). A crucial difference between delayed transfer marriage and other alternatives to major marriage like uxorilocal and minor marriage is that delayed transfer marriage was not an inferior marriage option within the major-marriage system. Delayed transfer marriage was itself the apex of an entirely distinct marriage system (henceforth, the "delayed transfer marriage system") that encompassed other inferior marriage forms—including secondary marriage and spirit marriage—but, significantly, not uxorilocal or minor marriage, neither of which was practiced within the delayed transfer area.

DELAYED TRANSFER MARRIAGE AND MARRIAGE RESISTANCE

Marjorie Topley argued in her landmark article, "Marriage Resistance in Rural Kwangtung," that the distinctive marriage practices of the Canton Delta constituted a form of "marriage resistance." Topley identified both a marrying and a nonmarrying form of marriage resistance: the *pu lo-chia*, wives who refused to cohabit with husbands, and the *tzu-shu nü*, women who refused to marry and instead took vows of spinsterhood. She analyzed these marriage-resistance practices in terms of local cultural and economic variables, attributing the rise of these practices primarily to the privileged economic position of women employed in the local silk industry.

My own research shows that Topley's analysis needs revision. Topley assumes that all local marriage practices that deviated from major marriage were marriage-resistance practices. My research shows that one of those distinctive practices—delayed transfer marriage—was not a form of marriage resistance, but rather the customary marriage pattern for an extensive area in the Canton Delta. There was indeed a marriage-resistance movement in the Delta, but one more limited in scope than that described by Topley. Some women of economic means did resist traditional marriage, but they were not rebelling against the constraints of major marriage. The Canton Delta marriage-resistance movement was composed of women in rebellion against the local delayed transfer marriage system. The peculiar forms of marriage resistance, unique in all of China, were shaped by the underlying delayed transfer marriage system. As is shown below, the marriage-resistance practices were the result of economic change working on the distinctive delayed transfer marriage system. In Chapters 7 and 8, I analyze the social and economic factors that contributed to the rise of the marriage-resistance practices in the delayed transfer area.

In the delayed transfer form of marriage, brides separated from their husbands on the third day after marriage and returned home to live with their natal families. By custom, brides were expected to live apart from their husbands for the first three years of marriage. During this initial period of "natolocal" residence, a bride was expected to visit her husband's family on the occasion of two or three festivals or family celebrations each year. The postmarital separation of husbands and wives was expected behavior and was described by informants as a "custom," like a "rule" or "regulation." All women marrying as first wives, whether from rich or from poor families, married with delayed transfer.

In delayed transfer marriages, the length of time that the spouses lived apart was to some extent influenced by individual circumstances, but informants reported that in most villages a separation of at least three years was expected (*jeui siu saam nihn sinji lohk ga*). Since the age at marriage for women in the delayed transfer area was 17 to 20, most brides were 20 or older when they finally settled in their husband's family home ("virilocal" residence). The most auspicious occasion for the entry of the bride as a resident spouse was a first pregnancy occurring about three years after marriage. Pregnancy always brought to a close the natolocal stage of marriage. An earlier pregnancy, and hence a premature close to the period of natolocal residence, brought a loss of prestige and social sanctions, especially ridicule by peers. Since marriage with delayed transfer was the cultural ideal, marriage with a shortened period of separation resembled marriage without delayed transfer, which in this marriage system was a less prestigious union. Thus, the delayed transfer form of marriage—characterized by a postmarital residence pattern for brides that anthropologists term "initial natolocal–delayed virilocal"—contrasted sharply with the orthodox major marriage with its ideal virilocal postmarital residence pattern. The separation of husband and wife after marriage—a practice reported as marriage resistance by Topley and interpreted by others as well as the effect of economic change on the major form of marriage—was, after all, the customary form of marriage in the Canton Delta.

RESEARCH AND WRITING METHODOLOGY

The research on which this study is based was initially conducted in Hong Kong in 1979–81 as my doctoral dissertation fieldwork for the Department of Anthropology at Stanford University. In 1986, I returned to Hong Kong to undertake more fieldwork as a postdoctoral project for the American Council of Learned Societies and the Center for Chinese Studies at the University of California, Berkeley. In Hong Kong, I interviewed more than 150 elderly women whose native villages lay in the Canton Delta. Typically, my informants emigrated to Hong Kong in the 1930's and 1940's in the wake of the severe political and economic disruptions occurring in the Canton Delta and throughout China at that time.* In Hong Kong, informants were located through their residence in vegetarian halls (*chai-t'ang*) for female lay practitioners of Buddhism, as well as in retirement homes and temporary housing shelters for the elderly.† All informants were interviewed at their place of residence. For this study, research in Hong Kong among Delta immigrants may well have been a more productive strategy than conducting a traditional field study in a Delta village. In Hong Kong vegetarian halls and retirement homes, I was able to draw on informants from more than 70 Canton Delta villages, concentrated mostly within four adjacent counties. In obtaining a regional perspective on local marriage practices, I was able to distinguish patterns in marriage and differentiate pattern from variation. Clearly emerging from the aggregate data were the outlines of the delayed transfer marriage system.

Retrospective interviews focused on marriage practices and labor patterns in the informants' native villages in the Canton Delta, on markets and schedules, male and female migration, crops and harvests, and men's and women's jobs by age, marital status, and postmarital residence. Other core interview questions focused on village marriage practices in the informant's own and immediately ascending generations. The interviews were designed to elicit information on temporal and spatial variation in marriage practices and economic roles, on how an informant, her agemates, paternal aunts, and grandmothers married and worked.

Since delayed transfer marriage was unknown to me at the outset, the interviews reflect the emerging direction of the research itself. Structured around the questions described above, interviews were regularly adjusted to incorporate new information and insights. New topics that began to figure significantly in the developing analysis—for example, "girls' houses" and their role in the socialization of girls in the delayed transfer mar-

---

*Especially the disruptions caused by the Chinese civil war and the collapse of the sericultural industry with the world depression.

†For more information on *chai-t'ang*, see Topley 1958, Sankar 1978, and Greenway 1987.

riage area—were explored in sections added to the interview schedule. Read chronologically, therefore, the interviews are characterized by a shifting emphasis, an alternate broadening and narrowing of focus, and an overall unfolding as the features of the delayed transfer marriage system became apparent.* The interviews were conducted in Cantonese. Although I had studied Cantonese for several years, I worked with a research assistant, Eunice Mei-wan Ku, for the entire period of research. The interviews were not recorded because informants were defensive about what they knew others considered an unorthodox practice and sensitive about topics such as the sexual behavior of wives in the early years of marriage. Therefore, we took notes during interviews, which we reviewed immediately afterward, using a tape recorder to preserve our discussion. From these written and taped notes of interviews, I constructed personal accounts. These accounts, which appear as illustrations throughout the following chapters, convey as closely as possible the information, emphasis, logic, and emotion communicated by the informant.

In this book, I describe delayed transfer marriage at a particular historical moment, from 1860 to 1930, when it was subject to economic changes that altered it. Although delayed transfer marriage occurred in both silk-producing ("sericultural") areas and in agricultural areas in the Canton Delta, developments in the sericultural industry figure prominently in my analysis of changes in the delayed transfer system. A primary focus of my analysis is the articulation of the systems of delayed transfer marriage and sericulture; these I describe as mutually shaping and constraining. I use personal accounts to balance my analysis, with a perspective on individuals as "actors" in these systems (Bourdieu 1977). Not only were informants' goals and strategies, as conveyed in these personal accounts, shaped by the systems of delayed transfer marriage and sericulture, but they in turn reshaped those systems. The personal accounts that appear in the following chapters show women transacting radi-

*For more on the development of my research, see Appendix A.

cal compensation marriages, boldly initiating spirit marriages, and running away to become sworn spinsters. They also show other women conforming to the traditional expectations of marriage in the delayed transfer system and settling in their husband's home after a few years of natolocal residence.

THE DELAYED TRANSFER MARRIAGE AREA

The region in which the delayed transfer marriage area is situated is one of the two great deltas of China (the other being the Yangtze Delta). The rich alluvial soils of the Canton Delta, formed into tracts or polders, are crosscut by myriad waterways. The Delta is the combined result of natural deposition by the East, West, and North rivers and of reclamation efforts. The powerful lineages for which the Canton Delta is noted organized the great business of land reclamation and built and maintained dikes. These lineages also organized the local sericultural industry, which established the Canton Delta as one of the great silk-producing regions of China. The sericultural heartland of the Canton Delta was wholly contained within the area in which delayed transfer marriage was practiced; delayed transfer marriage was, however, also practiced in agricultural areas where sericulture did not exist.*

On the basis of fieldwork, I have established delayed transfer marriage in seven counties in the Delta, including parts of Naahmhoi, Punyu, Jungsaan, Saamseui, Hoksaan, Dunggun,

*For a discussion of lineage organization in Kwangtung province and the Canton Delta, see Freedman 1958, 1966; and Potter 1970. For a critique of Freedman's and Potter's analyses, see Faure 1986, 166–79. On the Canton Delta sericultural industry, see Eng 1986, So 1986, and Chapter 8 below. Henceforth I use the broad terms *sericultural* and *agricultural* to distinguish those places or areas that practice sericulture, either exclusively or as part of a mixed economy, from places or areas that do not. Thus, a sericultural village may be one where silkworms are reared, mulberry groves cultivated, or silk reeled by any of the various technologies. I found in my research that places oriented toward the silk markets—whether egg, cocoon, mulberry, or raw-silk markets—had more in common culturally than did places oriented exclusively to other markets. I do not mean to suggest that all sericultural villages produced products exclusively for the silk markets. Many also produced rice and other crops or engaged extensively in other enterprises.

and all of Sundak (see Appendix C). In addition, on the basis of archival research, delayed transfer marriage can be established in one other Delta county, Goumihng (K'ai 1926). Map 1 shows the places where delayed transfer marriage is known to have been practiced. Villages practicing delayed transfer marriage tended to be contiguous and not randomly intermixed with villages practicing major marriage. It also appears that delayed transfer marriage was characteristic of some standard marketing communities and that those communities defined an area in which delayed transfer marriage was the rule.

A delayed transfer marriage "core area" within which no places practicing major marriage were reported lies primarily to the south of the city of Canton and includes all of Sundak county, and parts of Punyu, Naahmhoi, Jungsaan, Saamseui, and Hoksaan counties. The population of this core area probably reached several million in the early twentieth century.* Map 2 shows the delayed transfer core area as well as reported adjacent major-marriage areas. The informants themselves described a delayed transfer marriage area. Delta informants from both outside the delayed transfer area and outside any county containing that marriage form identified Sundak county as the heartland of the system. Informants from Naahmhoi county identified the Sai Tiuh area in Naahmhoi as a center of delayed transfer marriage. Punyu informants identified the lower part of that county as constituting the delayed transfer area. Jungsaan informants reported that the Siu Laahm area in the north practiced delayed transfer marriage, but that the Sehk Keih area in the south practiced major marriage exclusively. Informants from Toisaan and Sanwui counties and the New Territories of Hong Kong reported that delayed transfer marriage was not practiced in those areas.

For informants from within the delayed transfer marriage

---

*Establishing a more precise population figure is problematic since the area encompasses—in addition to Sundak—parts of seven counties. According to the 1853 edition of the *Gazetteer of Sundak County*, Sundak itself contained just over one million inhabitants toward the middle of the nineteenth century. By the early twentieth century, the sericultural part of the delayed transfer area alone contained more than two million people. See Chapter 8.

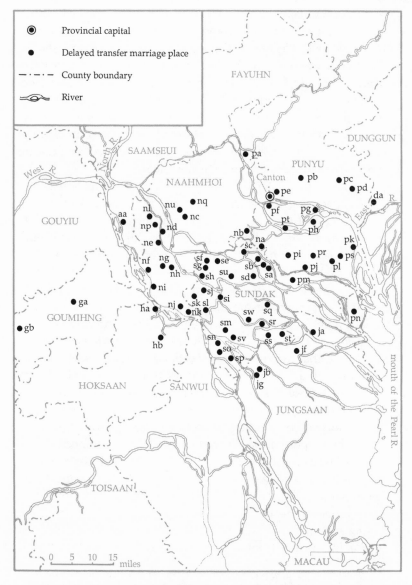

Map 1: The distribution of delayed transfer marriage places. See Appendix C for place-name identification.

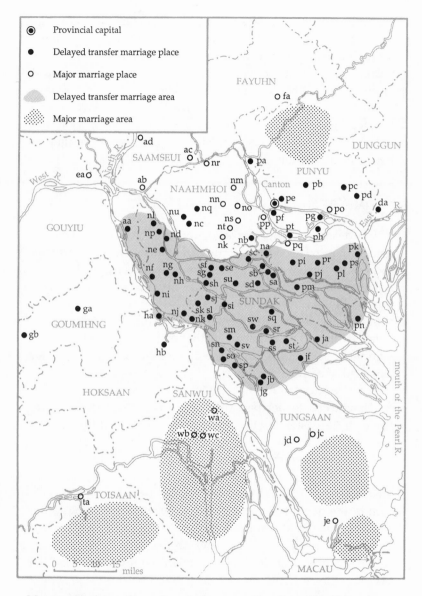

Map 2: The delayed transfer marriage area. See Appendix C for place-name identification.

system, marriage with delayed transfer was what they meant by the verb "to marry" (*gitfan*). To establish whether delayed transfer marriage or major marriage was practiced in an informant's village, I had to ask specifically about postmarital residence. Did brides settle with their husbands immediately after marriage (*yauh mouh jikhaak lohk ga*)?* An informant from a delayed transfer marriage village would explain that it was customary in her village for a bride to wait at least three years before settling in her husband's home.

FROM "BRIDEDAUGHTER" TO "WIFE"

Within delayed transfer marriage, the status of "married women" consisted in effect of two sequential statuses. Married women residing at home with their natal family in the early years of marriage I call "bridedaughters." Married women living in their husband's home in the later years of marriage I call "wives." Although here distinguished by residence, the two statuses also entailed distinctive behavior in the areas of production, consumption, sex, and reproduction. I first consider the behavior expected of a bridedaughter.

Shortly after the marriage rites (usually on the third day), a bride returned to her parents' home to continue in residence there for the customary three-year period. During this initial period of natolocal residence, a bridedaughter was required to make a few visits each year to her husband's home. In some places, the first conjugal visit customarily took place one month after marriage. Later visits were usually arranged on the occasion of the major festivals (the Lunar New Year, Ch'ing Ming, Dragonboat, and Mid-autumn festivals) or in some places on the occasion of family birthdays and anniversaries. (Some informants reported that the husband might be invited to visit the bridedaughter's home on special family occasions and would

---

*Of course, now—after the nature of the delayed transfer marriage system has been made clear—this question seems self-evident. But learning to ask this question, which happened for me during the course of one interview, quite simply changed the entire course of my research.

send his in-laws gifts of food at festival times.) The scheduling of conjugal visits to the husband's home was established by custom or set by the senior generation and arranged at the time of the marriage negotiations. In some places, an invitation from the husband's family was considered a prerequisite for a conjugal visit. In other places, informants described bridedaughters as visiting the husband's family "automatically" on prescribed occasions.

An 85-year-old informant from Hoksaan county explained that in her village, Siu Heung, near the market town Sya Pihng Heui, bridedaughters were expected to visit the husband's family twice every year until they *lohk ga*, or settled permanently in the husband's family home. Each year bridedaughters visited during the New Year's festival and at one other festival occasion, but a different one each year. In the first year of marriage, the bridedaughter visited only at the New Year, from New Year's eve through the third day of the festival, returning home on the fourth day. In the second year of marriage, she was required to visit at the New Year and during the Ch'ing Ming Festival. In the third, she visited at New Year's and at the Ghost Festival. In the fourth, at New Year's and on the Winter Solstice Festival. (If by the fifth year of marriage she hadn't already settled in her husband's family home, she was expected to do so then.) Before each visit, the husband's family formally invited the bridedaughter to come, sending a sedan chair for her, and a traditional gift for her family of peanuts wrapped in red cloth. The bridedaughter's family sent in return a red envelope containing a few cents, a traditional gift of good-luck money called *leihsih*.

By some accounts, invitations to visit were tantamount to summons that could not be refused. By other accounts, invitations could be refused and visits postponed. In some places, an invitation took the form of a gift or a basket of fruit or cakes sent by the mother-in-law to the mother of the bridedaughter; acceptance signaled agreement to the visit. Depending on family circumstances, a go-between might be employed to arrange a visit and a sedan chair engaged to convey the bridedaughter to her husband's home. In other cases, a bridedaughter simply walked to the husband's home, accompanied by a member of the husband's family.

Informants described bridedaughters as generally reluctant to visit their husband's family. Because delayed transfer marriages were blind matches, a conjugal visit was in essence an encounter between strangers. Husbands and wives were said to have no affection for one another on early visits. Informants called the back-and-forth of visiting "inconvenient," and observed that "of course, every woman wanted just to stay at home with her family." Some informants explained that married women were "afraid" of their mother-in-law. Others spoke of feeling "strange" with their husband, and even of there being much "anger" between spouses. A perceptive observer of this marriage system in the mid-nineteenth century, John Henry Gray, concluded that "these visits of ceremony are, I believe, very distasteful to Chinese brides" (1878, 1:208).* By some accounts, conjugal visits enabled a married woman to become better acquainted with her husband and his family before going to live with them. Some informants described a bridedaughter's permanent settling in her husband's home in terms of anger being resolved (*keuih nauyuhn la*).

Two accounts of conjugal visits provide ethnographic detail and suggest variation in the dynamics of delayed transfer marriage as practiced within sericultural as opposed to agricultural villages—and perhaps more generally, as practiced in more prosperous as opposed to less prosperous families.

The 65-year-old informant was from Lahm Ngohk in Naahmhoi, a multi-surname village near the silk center of

* Other descriptions of conjugal visits can be found in Tien 1952 and Fabre 1935. One of the best descriptions of conjugal visits within the delayed transfer system is given by K'ai Shih, who reports that in Goumihng county, wives lived separately from their husbands for several years after marriage, some returning after five to six years, some waiting until pregnancy, and all returning at the latest after eight to ten years (1926, 937–38).

Chahn Chyun.* Situated in the sericultural area, her village specialized in the silkworm-rearing phase of silk production. There were no steam-powered silk-reeling factories in Lahm Ngohk, but bridedaughters could earn money and accumulate savings by embroidering, reeling silk in small workshops, and weaving satin for local use. The informant explained that a bridedaughter could not go and live with her husband for several years after marriage or she would be scorned by her village "sisters," or *jimui*, her agemates.† In Lahm Ngohk, bridedaughters typically remained in their natal homes for at least three years, and usually for four to five years. During this time, she explained, although a bridedaughter was expected to visit her husband's family, her mother didn't want her to visit too often, only two or three times a year. In the beginning, it was customary for bridedaughters to demonstrate a reluctance to visit the husband's family, and even to refuse the first invitations to visit. The informant, who herself had married, described this behavior as a kind of "game." Usually a mother-in-law sent a sedan chair for her daughter-in-law when she wanted her to visit. The bridedaughter knew that if she did not refuse at least the first invitation, her "sisters" would sneer at her and even her mother-in-law would think less of her. Therefore, the bridedaughter paid off the sedan chair bearers out of her own pocket saying, "There! I've paid you! You tell them I won't

*Informants described their natal village as either multi- or single-surname settlements. Although single-surname villages were common in the delayed transfer area, Faure cautions against assuming that these villages were organized as single lineages (1986: 170–71). Single-surname villages were composed of families either from one lineage or from several lineages that shared the same surname. "Surname exogamy" was practiced in China; a shared surname presumed common family origins and persons from the same family were not permitted to marry. Thus, women born in single-surname villages were compelled to marry men from other villages and to settle permanently in another village; women from multi-surname villages could marry men from the same village and settle permanently in their natal village. The location of a husband's home had a considerable effect on a woman's ability to maintain ties to her family and female friends. For more on the relationship between a woman and her family and friends, both before and after marriage, see Chapter 2.

†For more on "sisters," see Chapter 2.

come!" The informant explained that although a bridedaughter usually visited on invitation, she was at first expected to make a show of her reluctance to go. This was "kind of fun." She also explained that when a bridedaughter did visit her husband, she treated him "like the enemy." By her account, bridedaughters and husbands routinely quarreled and then made up, and enjoyed this kind of play.

The 78-year-old married informant was from Fo Chyun in Punyu, one in a cluster of villages centering on the market town of Loh Gong. All villages in the cluster shared the same surname. This was a farming community, specializing in the cultivation of fruit trees, especially litchi. In Fo Chyun, bridedaughters were expected to help their parents farm, but received no wages for their work. The informant explained that even if a bridedaughter raised fruit to take to market, she returned home with rice or other provisions her family needed. Bridedaughters had no savings. When they left to live as wives in their husband's home, they helped the husband's family. Bridedaughters in Fo Chyun usually lived with their natal family for five to six years before settling in their husband's home. The informant observed that husbands didn't have to support their wives at first because they lived at home with their parents. When the husband's family extended an invitation to visit, a bridedaughter had to accept. Invitations were usually received in the afternoon or evening, and a bridedaughter would depart then, returning home the next morning. She said that in most cases there was no sedan chair, and a bridedaughter simply walked to her husband's home. A bridedaughter visited only on invitation, and if she didn't receive one, she wouldn't visit, sometimes for a whole year.*

---

*An interesting account of the organization of conjugal visits in Sundak—in an unnamed village—is given by Alfred Fabre, a Catholic priest. (Fabre provides one of the few descriptions of the delayed transfer system that is free of distortion.) In a discussion of the Ch'ing Ming festival (third day of the third month), which is devoted to honoring the dead, Fabre relates the unease created by a bridedaughter's visit to her husband at this time, as it would appear that she was

Of the behavior characterizing the status of bridedaughter, the pattern of sexual behavior was the most difficult to ascertain. How and when did the couple assume a sexual relationship? Because of both the sensitivity of the subject and the public setting in the vegetarian halls and retirement homes, informants were reluctant to discuss the sexual behavior of bridedaughters during the early years of marriage. However, three points are clear. Childlessness was a necessary condition for continued natolocal residence. The customary interval of natolocal residence was minimally about three years. Pregnancy was the most auspicious occasion for the entry of the bridedaughter into her husband's home as a virilocally resident wife. These conditions suggest that for most of the period between the marriage rites and the termination of natolocal residence—frequently in pregnancy—the sexual conduct of bridedaughters was aimed at the postponement of childbearing.

In the delayed transfer marriage area, social sanctions played a major role in encouraging delayed childbearing among bridedaughters. Informants, especially from sericultural villages, described how bridedaughters feared peer censure in the event of early pregnancy. In a typical comment, a Sundak woman explained, "If a bridedaughter became pregnant after being married only a short time, her 'sisters' would scorn her. They would say she really *wanted* to go and live with her husband! That's why bridedaughters tried to prevent pregnancy."

Some factors contributing to delayed childbearing were inherent in the structure of marriage itself, including the early separation of spouses and the infrequency and short duration of

---

confusing the living with the dead. She would be treating her husband, at least symbolically, as a dead person. In visiting, Fabre reports, a bridedaughter was required to follow a strict protocol, fixed by custom, which was to prepare her for ultimate cohabitation. She cohabited on the fifth day of the fifth month in the lunar calendar, the fifteenth day of the eighth month, at New Year, then at Ch'ing Ming, then again on the fifth of the fifth, the fifth of the eighth, at winter solstice, and then settled permanently in her husband's home at the New Year. Not to conform to this regime of visits was believed to bring bad luck, hence the saying "To cohabit first at winter solstice means barrenness, to cohabit next at the New Year means poverty, and to settle finally at Ch'ing Ming means the death of the husband." It seems clear that within the delayed transfer area, the organization of conjugal visits varied by place.

conjugal visits. Another factor was the growth of an anti-marital bias among young women in some places within the delayed transfer marriage area (see Chapter 7). In addition, interviews provide evidence of three methods of birth control practiced by bridedaughters: late consummation of marriage, avoidance of sexual intercourse, and termination of pregnancy. Although the impression given by informants is that there was a general tendency toward late consummation of marriage in the delayed transfer marriage area, accounts of bridedaughters who remained virgins for extended periods must be treated cautiously.

In some sericultural villages, as a result of an anti-marital bias and economic opportunities for bridedaughters, a radical variant of delayed transfer marriage gained popularity, a marriage-resistance practice that I call "compensation marriage" (see Chapter 3). In this departure from customary delayed transfer marriage, bridedaughters refused ever to consummate their marriages, negotiating a settlement with the husband's family that provided independence from husband and affines. My most articulate informants on the sexual behavior of bridedaughters proved to be either these compensating bridedaughters or sworn spinsters, women who practiced another radical alternative to customary delayed transfer marriage (see Chapter 4). Compensating bridedaughters and sworn spinsters told versions of a story about a bridedaughter who fought off her husband's advances for many years. As the story goes, this young woman would not even look at her husband when they were together at night and thus could not distinguish him from his brothers in the daytime.

In addition to the bias created by the relatively outspoken stance of the more radical women, the sensitivity of the subject of sexual behavior made it difficult to determine whether a certain behavior—for example, physical resistance—was employed to delay consummation of the marriage on the wedding night or as a routine measure to avoid sexual intercourse during subsequent conjugal visits. Most references to the means of delaying childbearing were, in fact, to a bridedaughter's resort to physical force. Ho It Chong, a sociologist who interviewed Canton Delta emigrants in Singapore in the 1950's, reports that certain organized groups of women in Sundak customarily resisted "any attempts by their husband to consummate marriage during the first two or three years of their married life" (1958, 37). However, it is difficult to judge from Ho's account whether this resistance was practiced primarily within organized groups or was more widespread in the general population of married women. Physical resistance to the consummation of marriage took different forms, including vigilance.

_____

The informant, from a rice-producing village in Punyu, explained that married women in her village usually lived with their parents for five to six years, but at the very least for three years. When a bridedaughter visited her husband's home, she didn't take any herbs to prevent pregnancy. She just sat upright, surrounded herself with furniture, and stayed awake all night!

_____

Bridedaughter status was further characterized by the claim of bridedaughters to support from their parents during the entire period of natolocal residence and the obligation of parents to provide it. A bridedaughter made no claim on her husband or affines for support of any kind during that period. Nowhere is this pattern of consumption more manifest than during conjugal visits. For the term of the visit, usually one to three days, the bridedaughter ate only food provided by her natal family and accepted no food from her husband's family. This dependence on provisions from her father's home during conjugal visits characterized the pattern of consumption for bridedaughters throughout the delayed transfer marriage area. When embarking on visits, bridedaughters took with them all the rice, oil, salt, tea, salted fish, sausages, and preserved eggs they would need during their stay. Some informants even reported taking firewood and water. While in their husband's home, bridedaughters cooked and ate their meals separately from the rest of the family. The particular arrangements for provisioning the bridedaughter on conjugal visits were made at the time of the marriage negotiations. Sometimes the natal family arranged for food to be delivered to the visiting bridedaughter by a local restaurant or a relative living in the husband's village. In one frequently mentioned arrangement, the natal family sent a personal maid (*gansan*) to accompany the bridedaughter, carry her basket of provisions, and prepare her meals.

This pattern of consumption was established behavior for bridedaughters and was expected by both families. Becoming a consumer in the husband's home symbolized the beginning of the shift from natolocal to virilocal residence for the bridedaughter. After several years, when the husband's family wanted the bridedaughter to move into their home, they began to urge her to eat with them. Her acceptance of food signaled that she would soon return to them as a resident wife. As one Punyu informant commented, "If you ate with the husband's family during visits, then your mother-in-law would ask for more frequent visits and expect you to settle with them soon. You didn't want to give her that idea!" Typically, a bridedaughter began to eat with her husband's family only after several years, beginning "gradually" and "eating just a little."

In general, women in the delayed transfer marriage system seemed more actively engaged in labor of all kinds, including field labor, than women in the major-marriage system. However, until a married woman entered her husband's home as a virilocally resident wife, neither her husband nor his family could lay claim to her labor or its products. Within their natal homes, bridedaughters usually performed the same economic roles as their unmarried sisters of similar age. In general, a woman's economic role changed significantly not at marriage itself but only at her assumption of virilocal residence. The tasks performed by bridedaughters varied widely over the delayed transfer marriage area; the most frequently reported were doing general household and farm chores, planting rice, reeling silk, weaving cloth, embroidering, and harvesting mulberry leaves. Whatever the task, however, the labor of bridedaughters benefited only her own family. In fact, the economic contribution of bridedaughters was commonly referred to as "helping parents."

Regardless of whether her labor was general or specialized in nature, whether its value was absorbed directly in the general household economy or realized as income, a bridedaughter's labor was claimed only by her natal family.

In villages where a bridedaughter worked for wages, her earnings went to help her own family, which housed and fed her, but she was usually permitted to keep part of her earnings for herself. Informants explained that the first priority was helping parents and that the economic situation of her natal family determined whether a bridedaughter saved anything for herself. However, bridedaughters did accumulate savings, which constituted a kind of private property for married women in the delayed transfer marriage area. When a bridedaughter went to live with her husband's family, she took this private property with her. It was not considered part of the dowry, which had been exchanged at marriage. Informants reported that a wife did not surrender her private property to her mother-in-law, but kept it and managed it herself. She used her private property, among other things, to help her husband out of financial difficulty.

A Sundak informant explained that when a bridedaughter went to live with her husband's family, she took all the property she had acquired with her own wages, including gold and silver jewelry and clothes. Although her first responsibility was to help her family, a bridedaughter usually managed to save some of her earnings for herself. Sometimes a bridedaughter was able to accumulate a big box of clothes, and then when she settled with her husband's family, she didn't need to ask them to make clothes for her. The informant explained that all the property a bridedaughter took with her was hers alone and was not appropriated by the mother-in-law. She stressed that this property was not given by parents, but was acquired with a bridedaughter's own earnings.

During a conjugal visit, a bridedaughter did not cook or do chores for her husband's family. She was expected, however, to burn incense for the husband's ancestors at the domestic altar and to serve tea to her mother-in-law. (If a bridedaughter was accompanied on her visit by a maid, the maid assisted her in the ritual of serving tea and rose early in the morning to light the incense for her.) When the mother-in-law urged the bridedaughter to cook for her husband's family, a bridedaughter refused unless she wanted to indicate that she would soon come to live with them. Hence, it was customary that a bridedaughter not cook for the first few years of marriage.

A Sundak informant explained that if the mother-in-law asked her to cook during a conjugal visit, a bridedaughter refused if she didn't want to settle in her husband's home yet. However, if the mother-in-law persisted, urging her to cook on every visit, then the bridedaughter had to begin cooking and preparing to settle in her husband's family.

The bridedaughter's assumption of cooking chores and other domestic responsibilities during a conjugal visit was a powerful symbolic gesture indicating the bridedaughter's acceptance of the authority of her mother-in-law and her readiness to assume the role of wife.

The underlying principle in the patterns of residence, sexual behavior, consumption, and production that characterized the behavior of bridedaughters is clearly that a bridedaughter's primary obligation was toward her parents and not her parents-in-law. Parents maintained authority over their married daughter for the first few years of marriage, claiming her obedience and labor and providing shelter and support until she settled in her husband's family.

Bridedaughters did, however, eventually become wives. This temporal relationship can be used to construct a paradigm of marriage as a process. In the delayed transfer system, "marriage," initiated by the wedding rites, was a process that brought a transition in status from bridedaughter to wife over a period of several years. This transition was marked by a shift in behavior from patterns appropriate to the status of a bridedaughter to those appropriate to a wife.

The completion of the marriage process brought major changes to the lives of married women. Bridedaughters in their natal homes, especially in sericultural villages, enjoyed considerable leverage with parents and marked prestige. The 1853 Sundak county gazetteer observed that married women experienced few restrictions on returning to live in their natal homes. Women in the delayed transfer marriage area—compared with women in major-marriage areas—enjoyed relatively lengthy residence in their natal villages. As girls, they formed close bonds with their village agemates, or "sisters," through participation in girls' houses and festival associations. Close friendships between women were a feature of the distinctive women's community in the delayed transfer area, a subject explored in the next chapter.

When a bridedaughter settled at last in her husband's home, she lost the freedoms and friendships that had been central to her life in her father's village. In her husband's home, a wife had to submit to the authority of her mother-in-law, to serve and obey her. A newly settled wife struggled under a heavy burden of domestic chores and severe restrictions on her behavior and activities. To visit her own family, a wife had to request permission repeatedly from her mother-in-law, who would allow her to visit only infrequently and for only one day at a time. As one married informant described the scenario, "If you wanted to visit your family, you had to serve tea to your mother-in-law. If she didn't like the kind of tea you served, then she wouldn't let you go. Sometimes even if she liked the tea you served her, she still wouldn't let you go!"

For many bridedaughters, perhaps most, the transition in status from bridedaughter to wife was initiated by pregnancy, which in effect completed the marriage process. Pregnant bridedaughters were expected to leave their natal homes before the birth of the child, but they usually stayed until late in their pregnancy. A few women reported measures taken by bridedaughters to prevent conception or terminate pregnancy, and thus forestall virilocal residence. These measures included drinking a solution of dried peach sap and water—red in color—on return from a conjugal visit, drinking a cup of water that had been poured over an iron nail, heated until red in color, and taking various red-colored herbal medicines. Unfortunately the data are too sparse to conclude that bridedaughters commonly resorted to these measures.

A Naahmhoi informant, from Lahm Ngohk, a sericultural village, recounted the experience of her second eldest sister, an accomplished silk reeler who earned a good wage. This sister was married and had lived apart from her husband for seven or eight years when she became pregnant. She didn't want to settle down with her husband just then, but wished to continue living at home and working as a silk reeler. Therefore, she went to gather herbs in the hills for the purpose of preparing a medicine, red in color, that would cause her to lose the child. Although she became ill and fainted on taking the medicine, her pregnancy continued. She finally left her natal home in the ninth month of pregnancy, taking with her to her husband's home substantial savings she had accumulated as a silk reeler. The baby was born weighing only three catties [about 4.5 pounds]. The informant explained that silk reelers didn't want to settle down with their husbands and that was why they took a lot of herbal medicines.

The end of the period of natolocal residence and postponement of childbearing meant the assumption of new tasks. The most marked changes in economic role for a married woman occurred at the end of the marriage process with the beginning of childbearing (see Chapter 8). The shift in the pattern of production that had begun with helping the mother-in-law cook during conjugal visits was accomplished on the bridedaughter's permanent transfer to her husband's home and her assumption of domestic labor and childbearing responsibilities. The completion of the marriage process in the transition from bridedaughter to wife brought to a close the period in a woman's life cycle when her primary obligation was to her own parents. No longer could a natal family claim their daughter's labor, and no longer were they obliged to provide her with material support.

Although informants cited pregnancy as the most common occasion for the transfer of the bridedaughter to her husband's home as a resident wife, other factors contributed to the length of the marriage process. Bridedaughters and their husbands were ultimately under the authority of parents, who were motivated for different reasons to lengthen or shorten the marriage process through the extension or curtailment of the period of natolocal residence. Since much of the discussion in the following chapters focuses on the attempt by natal families to retain the labor of economically valuable daughters in sericultural villages, it is instructive to consider examples, primarily from agricultural villages, in which natal families were motivated to shorten the marriage process. During times of economic hardship or political instability, the benefits of retaining a bridedaughter for her labor were outweighed by the cost and responsibility of keeping her.

The informant was from a single-surname village in the Sai Tiuh area of Naahmhoi. Villagers cultivated rice and sugarcane, and girls helped parents farm. The informant described how bridedaughters did not immediately settle down with their husbands after marriage, but remained at home with their parents for at least one to two years. That was the custom. However, a bridedaughter's parents had the authority to tell her to go and live with her husband at any time. According to the informant, parents in her village told a bridedaughter to leave early when there was no food at home.

Another Naahmhoi informant was also from a single-surname village in Sai Tiuh in Naahmhoi. Villagers cultivated primarily rice and turnips, and girls traditionally helped their parents farm. The informant explained that bridedaughters usually stayed with their parents from three to four years, assuming residence with their husband on pregnancy. However, the informant herself was told to settle with her husband only a short time after marriage. She explained that she had been married at 16 and had stayed with her parents for only a year and a half when a series of robberies took place in the village. Her mother feared for her safety and therefore sent her to live with her husband before the usual time.

Informants' accounts suggest that in addition the relative power of the families of the bridedaughter and husband figured in the length of intervals of separation. Some accounts describe how the husband's family "demanded," "ordered," or "pushed" the bridedaughter to settle with them. For example, an informant from Sya Wan in Punyu explained that bridedaughters stayed with their parents for three to six years after marriage until the husband's family "demanded" they live with them. "If the husband's family kept demanding that a bridedaughter settle, then she had to go." Another informant, from Siu Laahm in Jungsaan county, recounted how bridedaughters assumed residence with their husband after a few years, when the husband's family "forced" them to go. "The husband's family could force the bridedaughter to settle with them even though she wasn't pregnant. They pressured her parents, and then if she didn't come, the husband's family 'pursued' her parents!" Such accounts point to the dynamics between the family of the bridedaughter and that of her husband as important determinants of the interval of separation. These dynamics were undoubtedly shaped by the relative power and status not only of the individual families but also of the greater kinship units in which they were embedded, that is, the lineages to which the families belonged. As noted earlier, the Canton Delta was characterized by powerful lineages. For the husband's family, membership in a lineage more powerful than that of the bride's family must have meant that they could effectively pressure a family into surrendering their bridedaughter on demand. Was it the case that the greater the relative power and status enjoyed by the husband's family, the less likely the period of separation was terminated only by pregnancy? Unfortunately, the family and lineage dynamics of delayed transfer marriages may elude efforts to reconstruct them.

Although my research does not allow me to answer these larger questions, it does show that short intervals of separation were less prestigious. For a bridedaughter's parents, shorter than customary periods of natolocal residence had the effect of cutting short the time during which they continued to be responsible for their daughters. Short intervals, therefore, reflected a natal family's inability to support a bridedaughter or their social powerlessness vis-à-vis the husband's family. In addition, short intervals as a result of early pregnancy showed a bridedaughter's (and her natal family's) shameless disregard for local custom.* Whatever the reason, another factor contributing to the low prestige of short intervals of natolocal residence was that marriage without delayed transfer was in this marriage system the mark of another, inferior form of marriage, "secondary marriage."

SECONDARY MARRIAGE

One alternative form of marriage encompassed by the delayed transfer marriage system entailed no delayed transfer. This form, secondary marriage, was not a competing or desirable alternative to marriage with delayed transfer. Brides marrying as secondary wives married grooms who had previously married first wives with delayed transfer. Although an inferior match, a secondary marriage was not concubinage but a recognized marriage that produced legitimate children. Perhaps the fundamental difference between primary marriages with delayed transfer and secondary marriages without delayed transfer lay in the social origin of the brides themselves. Women marrying as second-

---

*K'ai Shih reports that in Goumihng county short intervals of postmarital separation were seen as less prestigious, and wives who returned to their husbands after only one or two years were sneered at by their peers (1926, 938).

ary wives formed a distinct social class; they were women who had as young girls been sold by their families into domestic servitude. These girls were called *muijai* (usually romanized *mui tsai*). In the wake of a flood, bad harvest, or drought, families were sometimes forced to sell their daughters to survive. Informants often described their villages as primarily muijai-givers or muijai-takers. From these descriptions emerges a picture of rural families in times of hardship selling daughters to employers in towns. A Sundak informant from urban Daaih Leuhng remembered that silk center as having a lot of muijai. After a bad harvest, villagers would sell their daughters in Canton and big towns like Daaih Leuhng. According to the informant, the sale brought a poor family enough cash to buy seed again.

Girls bought as muijai, called purchased girls (*maaih mui*), were generally about 10 years old, but always at least 7 and old enough to perform domestic services. Families sometimes pawned rather than sold their daughters as muijai. Called *dong mui*, pawned muijai brought their parents only half the sum brought by daughters who were sold. Whether sold or pawned, a deed of transfer was customary. In the case of pawned muijai, deeds specified the number of years before their families could redeem them. Parents, not the employer, were responsible for arranging the marriage of a pawned muijai. However, daughters were usually sold rather than pawned as muijai, thereby bringing a greater sum to their economically pressed parents and transferring the responsibility and expense of arranging their marriage to the employer.

In the employer's household, the role of the muijai was to serve family members. Although it became quite popular in some places for sworn spinsters to purchase muijai and train them to work in silk production, muijai acquired by families performed less specialized tasks, doing domestic chores and caring for family members. One Sundak informant from a village in Gong Meih recalled how virtually any village girl could learn to reel silk—with the exception of muijai, who had to serve their employers and had no time to reel silk. One variety of muijai was the personal maid, or *gansan,* who customarily accompanied a bridedaughter on conjugal visits.

The difference in life cycles for a family's own daughters and muijai was manifest in the marriage experience itself. Daughters, marrying with delayed transfer at age 17 to 20, enjoyed at least a three-year period of postmarital natolocal residence before settling in their husband's home, generally past the age of 20. A daughter's marital experience was one of both delayed virilocal residence and delayed childbearing. Muijai, by contrast, customarily married at 16, marrying directly from their employer's home to their husband's home and assuming immediate virilocal residence. Thus, secondary wives were compelled to assume the claims and obligations that defined the status of wife several years earlier than were bridedaughters.

Most informants reported that muijai invariably married as secondary wives. A few informants recalled cases in which a poor family acquired a muijai as a first wife for their son. However, in such uncommon cases, a muijai still assumed immediate virilocal residence.

The prestigious form of delayed transfer marriage entailed the exchange of both bridewealth and dowry. Contributing to the low prestige of secondary marriages was the exchange of bridewealth for, at best, only a token dowry, which typified such marriages. With marriage payments flowing primarily in one direction, from bride-takers to bride-givers, a secondary marriage resembled the outright purchase of the bride. In fact, the commercial character of secondary marriages was reflected in the practice of investing in muijai for later sale as secondary wives. As one spinster explained, "If you had a pretty muijai, when you married her off, she brought you more cakes, pork, and bridewealth."

The lower prestige of secondary marriages was reflected in the absence of the symbols associated with delayed transfer marriages. Informants reported that when employers married muijai out as secondary wives, they did not customarily send along a bridal quilt, an essential dowry item in delayed transfer marriages. Nor could the festive red sedan chairs (*daaih huhng fa giu*) used by brides in delayed transfer marriages be used by brides in secondary marriages; they rode instead in green sedan chairs (*ching yi giu*). Thus, onlookers could readily distinguish between first and secondary wives. Those informants who recalled cases in which a muijai had married as first wife described a third type of sedan chair, a plain wooden one (*muhk tauh giu*), which conveyed both the bride and the social message that this was a muijai marrying as a first wife.

Within the delayed transfer marriage system, many secondary wives were acquired under a radical arrangement—compensation marriage—in which a bridedaughter contracted out to a secondary wife some of the claims and obligations of marriage. But before turning to a discussion of compensation marriage, the first of several marriage-resistance practices discussed here, we need to take a closer look at some of the distinctive features of the society in which these practices flourished.

2

The Girls' House and the Women's Community

As I slowly worked out the dimensions of the delayed transfer marriage system—a system that appears in its arrangements and social dynamics so different from those of the major-marriage system in traditional Chinese society—I began to notice other distinctive features of the social landscape in the Canton Delta. Among these were girls' houses and, more rarely, boys' houses (separate residences for adolescent girls and boys) and the practice of marriage at night. I was gradually driven to the working hypothesis that these practices were part of an older, non-Chinese cultural complex, one that fused with Chinese culture to produce the distinctive version of Chinese society found in the Canton Delta. I say more about this hypothesis in the Conclusion. In this chapter I discuss the unique women's community in the delayed transfer area, a community characterized by girls' houses, the staging of important community festivals by young unmarried women, and the formation of strong bonds between women who were from the same village, that is, village daughters.

Elsewhere in traditional Chinese society, the primary women's community was created by ties of marriage; it was located in the husband's village and composed of women who had married in as wives. Margery Wolf has provided a classic description of this kind of women's community in Taiwan (1972, 32–52). In the delayed transfer area, however, the primary women's community was created by ties of birth; it was located in father's village and composed of women who were village daughters. Because marriage usually entailed at least three years of natolocal residence for brides, women in the delayed transfer area spent twenty years or more as daughters in their father's family. This lengthy tenure as daughter was shaped by a distinctive socialization experience structured largely around the girls' house.

THE ORGANIZATION OF GIRLS' HOUSES

The following account of a girls' house was provided by an 85-year-old woman from Siu Heung village in Hoksaan county. The account elucidates some features common to the organization of girls' houses in most places in the delayed transfer marriage area and others peculiar to the informant's own village. Although situated within the delayed transfer area, Siu Heung lay outside the area in which the radical practice of compensation marriage occurred. The informant's account therefore describes the girls' house tradition in a conservative village.

The informant married with delayed transfer at age 18 and settled down with her husband and his family after four years, at the age of 22. In Siu Heung, it was the custom for adolescent girls to sleep apart from their families together in a girls' house. Typically five to seven girls stayed in one girls' house, which was an empty or extra village house that was made available rent-free to the girls. All girls took meals with their families and worked at home during the day, returning to the girls' house only to sleep. According to the informant, girls in the girls' house were very close. They spent the eve-

nings chatting, doing a little sewing or embroidery, and play-
ing games like dominoes. It wasn't important for all the girls
of one house to be from the same family or share the same
surname. Her village had four different surnames, so girls
from different families stayed together. Bridedaughters visited their friends at the girls' house and could stay there, too.
In her particular girls' house, all the girls aimed to be very
tidy. Fines were levied if anyone left a mess or found dirt or a
stray thread on someone's clothes. The money from these
fines was saved. Later, when all five girls in her girls' house
married, they held a "wish fulfillment" banquet to thank the
gods for their good fortune. The money collected from fines
was used to make gold earrings for each girl, and to pay for
the banquet itself. The girls hired blind men to sing ballads
on the eve of the banquet. They invited neighbors and family
members to attend, as well as former residents of the house,
who were now married women with children.

As the older girls one by one left the house, younger girls
were recruited as new members. At first, a new girl did only
simple chores like washing cups, boiling water, or sweeping
the floor. Always, the informant recalled, they tried to have
five girls staying in her girls' house.

———

The girls' house, or its functional equivalent, was widely
distributed throughout the Canton Delta.* The delayed transfer
marriage area was contained within a more extensive area in
which girls' houses were traditional. The evidence suggests that
girls' houses occurred in a broad band from the Sz Yap counties
(four counties to the southeast), across the delayed transfer marriage area and the lower half of Jungsaan county, and into Dunggun and Boungon counties and the New Territories of Hong

———

*"Boys' houses" also occurred throughout this same area, although their
distribution is even less certain than that of girls' houses. Boys' houses have
been reported only very occasionally in the delayed transfer marriage area. See
the Conclusion. See also Spencer and Barrett 1948 for a discussion of "bachelor
houses" in a village in Jungsaan county. Parish and Whyte report that "youth
houses," including "male rooms," still existed in some Canton Delta villages in
the 1970's (1978, 231–32).

Kong. Unfortunately, we have insufficient data to determine how continuous this broad belt was. My field research shows that within the delayed transfer marriage area, girls' houses occurred in virtually all informants' villages, and they can therefore be considered a regular feature of that marriage system.

In the delayed transfer marriage area, girls' houses provided a gathering place and separate sleeping accommodations for girls, beginning in early adolescence. Girls' houses were usually not specially built; typically they were empty or extra houses, owned by families and situated on family land. They were not owned by the girls themselves, nor were they established beyond village boundaries, distinctions whose significance will become apparent later in the discussion of the radical "spinster houses." According to informants, typically eight to ten girls belonged to one girls' house. Larger houses, however, were known: one of my informants reported twenty girls in one house, and Topley reported forty in another (1973, 9).

In the delayed transfer marriage area, three basic organizational configurations of girls' houses can be distinguished. In the first variation, girls worked at home during the day, took meals with their family, and spent each night in the girls' house. In a slight modification of this configuration, informants from some places reported that girls spent every night in the girls' house except during festivals, when they returned home to stay with their family.

In the second configuration, girls worked at home during the day and spent only occasional nights in the girls' house, perhaps a few nights a month. Sometimes girls took their meals at home; at other times they proceeded directly from work to the girls' house to cook and eat together. Informants described girls as deciding for themselves when they would stay in the girls' house and whether they would cook together or eat at home. According to informants, girls might decide just to gather in the girls' house after work to visit and then return home to sleep, "whatever they liked."

In the last configuration, an older woman or widow, living alone and desiring companionship, invited a few girls to stay with her. This variation seemed to occur less frequently within the delayed transfer marriage area than in some places outside. To take one example, an informant from Lahm Ngohk in Naahmhoi county in the delayed transfer area described girls' houses there as typically extra or empty houses; sometimes, however, an older woman who was living alone and wanted company invited girls to come stay with her. By contrast, informants from a part of Dunggun county that was outside the delayed transfer area described the widow-centered house as the model for girls' houses in that area. One Dunggun informant remarked, "Widows loved having girls stay with them and invited them to come. The noise made the house lively!"* In all three variations, girls' lives were organized around the back-and-forth rhythm of days at home and work and nights, regularly or occasionally, spent at the girls' house.

Not every girl, however, belonged to a girls' house. Muijai—the young servant girls introduced in the last chapter—were excluded from membership. Informants reported exceptional cases in which a "good" employer chose to treat a muijai "like an adopted daughter" and permitted her to stay in the girls' house. Usually, however, muijai were described as so busy with household chores and serving family members that they had no time to spend in a girls' house. As one informant explained, "Very few muijai had a chance to sleep in the girls' house. Each muijai was looked after by a particular family member, who didn't want her to go out too often. People were afraid muijai would learn bad habits in the girls' house and not want to return to work." The girls' house was the domain of village girls who were raised as daughters, not muijai.

For daughters, the primary criterion for membership in a girls' house seemed to be either friendship with other members or an early introduction to the house through a relative who belonged, especially an elder sister or a paternal aunt. As an informant from the multi-surname village of Lahm Ngohk in Naahmhoi elaborated, "There were several girls' houses in Lahm

*For a description of widow-centered girls' houses in a contemporary village in the Canton Delta, see Chan et al. 1984, 164–65.

Ngohk. Girls liked to group together. If an elder sister was staying in one girls' house, then her younger sister might like to go there, too. If father's sister was staying in a girls' house, she might bring along her niece. That's how girls grouped together in the girls' house."

Membership in a girls' house was not restricted to girls of only one family except under special circumstances. Of course, in single-surname villages, girls in the girls' house were from the same "family"; that is, they were sisters, cousins, paternal aunts, nieces, and other more distant relatives sharing the same family name. In some cases, a girls' house was not the typical extra or empty house but a special house designated by an ancestor as a girls' house and passed down from generation to generation. In this special case, the house was used by girls from only that family. (It is tempting to speculate that perhaps at one time—or ideally—girls' houses were more closely identified with one particular family or lineage.)

Informants were quick to point out that membership in a girls' house did not entail an entrance fee, rent payments, or an economic contribution of any kind. In addition, membership in a girls' house was not restricted to girls of one economic class or background. Informants described girls from rich and from poor families as grouping together in the girls' houses.

Surprisingly, informants reported that girls' houses had no adult chaperone, with, of course, the exception of the widow-centered girls' houses. When asked why parents did not object to girls' staying together unsupervised, informants unanimously responded that parents had no objections because it was a "custom," a "regulation," for girls to stay together in the girls' house. "Girls were all very independent and free." "Girls at that time were all well behaved." I was assured that, of course, parents knew both when girls were planning to stay in the girls' house and who the other members were.

In most places in the delayed transfer marriage area, girls' houses were known as *neuihjai nguk* (literally "girls' houses"). They were also known by several other names, however, which made research problematic.* Further complicating the picture was a tendency in prosperous villages and towns for girls' houses to merge with another institution, the radical "spinster house" (*gupoh nguk*) to produce a variant defined less by the age of its occupants than by their marital status (see Chapters 4 and 7). A few places in the sericultural area had no girls' houses because empty houses were used as dormitories for female silk workers from neighboring villages. But even in places with no formal girls' houses, there was much visiting between girls of different households and families. Informants reported that it was customary for several girls to rotate among families, spending a few nights with each. In still other places with no formal girls' houses, girls slept "upstairs" in the loft apart from the rest of the family. Although there was much variation, virtually every place in the delayed transfer marriage area made some kind of arrangement for at least the occasional separate accommodation of adolescent girls.

GIRLS' HOUSES AND SOCIALIZATION

Girls' houses did not have a primarily economic function. Although in the evenings girls sometimes engaged in such tasks as embroidering, sewing, and weaving to earn extra income, these were neither regular nor organized endeavors. A few informants gave examples of girls' houses serving as workshops, but these were rare. Activities in the girls' houses were typically described as primarily social. Informants recounted how girls gathered in the evening in the girls' house to talk, tell stories, play games, and sing ballads. Anthropologist Andrea Sankar relates an informant's personal account that illustrates some of the activities and dynamics of life in the girls' house:

*In the delayed transfer area, girls' houses were also called *kwahndeuih nguk* and *muijai nguk*. Outside the delayed transfer area in the New Territories of Hong Kong, girls' houses were called *mah nguk* (David Faure, personal communication). Parish and Whyte provide still other names from their interviews with Canton Delta immigrants (1978, 231).

In my district, P'an-yü [Punyu], all girls live in girls' houses. This is because their homes are so small that they will see their father and brothers using the chamber pot at night, and this would be terribly embarrassing. Therefore, we spent the night with only other girls. We moved into the house as soon as we could take care of ourselves at night or when we reached puberty. All the girls wanted to live in the girls' house; it was great fun.

The girls ate at home and worked with their families. Some did agricultural work; some did housework. After dinner the girls would gather at the girls' house to chat and play. . . . Girls under ten, who are not yet members, serve the older members by, for instance, fanning them. The younger girls also learn the skills of embroidery at this time. At nine o'clock we went into a large communal bedroom. We were supposed to sleep but we continued to work by candlelight and talk. Each house had ten or more members. All the parents thought that the girls' houses were a good thing. (Sankar 1978, 109–10)

When pressed for an explanation why there were girls' houses, most of my informants replied with what I came to regard as a stock response, "girls enjoyed grouping together" (*di neuihjai hou jungyi kwahnmaaih yatchai*). Some informants said that young girls didn't like to stay with adults, preferring to group together on their own. A few mentioned a lack of sleeping room and privacy at home. Although the girls' house most certainly alleviated crowding at home, it is significant that informants emphasized female companionship as the primary rationale for the girls' houses.

The chatting and gossiping in the evenings in the girls' house were not only entertainment, but served important communication purposes as well. Girls talked about almost everything, an informant from Sya Gau in Sundak reminisced, but mostly they enjoyed gossiping about which parents were arranging marriages. Since marriage arrangements in the delayed transfer marriage area were quietly negotiated between the elders of the two families, without the knowledge of the future bride, a girl depended on the watchful eyes of her friends. Any unusual domestic events observed while she was away from home—for example, the arrival of visitors or gifts—might signal an impending engagement. In places where radical marriage-resistance practices occurred, advance warning of an impending marriage gave a girl time to set in motion alternative marriage strategies. A soon-to-be-engaged girl from a sericultural area might, for instance, decide to run away to become a sworn spinster, or she might initiate negotiations for a compensation marriage. Of course, most girls in the delayed transfer area pursued a more traditional course of action, submitting to the authority of their parents in the matter of marriage, with a good measure of commiseration from friends.

The evening exchange of stories and ballads in the girls' house played an important role in the socialization of women in the delayed transfer area. In some places, this socialization took the form of explicit instruction in manners. One Naahmhoi informant explained that girls' houses in her village were typically owned by wealthy men and used by their daughters, who invited other unmarried girls to play and stay with them. These daughters of the wealthy taught the other girls "manners" (hohk leihmauh). Most informants described a more informal learning situation in the girls' house, one dependent on mutual assistance. One girl would teach another something she knew—for instance, how to write characters—and the other would in turn teach her something. Although I was unable to collect systematic data on female literacy, the impression given me by informants is that it was not uncommon for girls in the delayed transfer area to receive at least some basic instruction. Many of the ballads popular in the girls' house were in print and circulated widely among girls. Some informants told how girls were formally tutored together off the main room of the ancestral hall. (Boys were tutored in the main room.) Other informants described a more informal setting in the girls' house for acquiring rudimentary literacy. The following account by a Sundak woman, an informant of Sankar's, allows further insight into the various learning experiences provided by the girls' house:

All the girls in my village joined the girls' house. You learned nothing if you did not join the girls' house. In school teachers taught only things in books. They never taught you any girls' secrets like menstruating and marriage. In the girls' house you also learned important things like how to cry for a sister when she got married. This crying was very important and a girl's sisters had to do it; there are special things one must say at a marriage. The girls learn embroidery at the girls' house. No money was required to join.

The girls in the girls' house read the three-character classics, which are books about Confucius, and sang songs. Some of the songs had no words; some were about the problems of being a woman or of being a sou hei [sworn spinster]. There was no head of the house. The girls shared the expenses and work.

Sometimes the members of a girls' house would try to prevent the marriage of one of their sisters. They would try to help the bride-to-be escape, but rarely with success. Usually the family of the girl to be married would lock her up with her sisters for several days before the wedding and let them all cry and sing together.

I did not have to decide which girls' house to join. Usually there was a group of five or six girls who lived on the same alley and played together. Often they were cousins. One decided to go into the girls' house and soon another followed and the number grew in no time; it was very easy. Unlike Hong Kong, everyone in the village was close. Everybody left their doors open; girls got to know each other very well. Usually the whole village had the same last name. If there were not enough beds in the girls' house, some girls would return to sleep at home around ten; otherwise, everyone spent the night there. (Sankar 1978, 104–5)

The girls' house as an important agent of socialization gave a decidedly different shape to the lives of girls in the delayed transfer marriage area. One effect of the girls' house experience was to promote close bonds between unmarried girls. Girls from the same girls' house considered themselves "sisters" (*jimui*).* Sometimes girls formalized this relationship with pledges and a banquet attended by friends and family members. There has been a tendency in the Chinese literature to cast the close relationships between girls in this area as homosexual in character (see, e.g., K'ai 1926, 938–39; Ch'en 1933, 300; Hu 1936, 34). My own research did not specifically address this issue, but two facts must be taken into consideration when evaluating such comments on delayed transfer marriage. As discussed at greater

Jimui in single-surname villages were often sisters, paternal aunts, cousins, and nieces, as well as more distant relatives sharing the same family name.

length in Chapter 6, the unorthodox delayed transfer form of marriage has long been subject both to the cultural biases of Chinese outside that marriage system and to governmental repression. Thus, when receiving formal attention in the literature at all, delayed transfer marriage is described in a distorted manner and cast as politically dangerous. In a parallel manner, women practicing this form of marriage are typically portrayed in this literature as morally scandalous, that is, as "loose" or "lesbian."*

STAGING THE DOUBLE SEVEN FESTIVAL

The close bonds between unmarried girls formed the basis of a distinctive women's community in the delayed transfer area. Although the girls' house may have provided the original stimulus, close relationships between girls found expression and reinforcement in other experiences as well. The Double Seven festival, climaxing on the seventh day of the seventh month of the lunar year, was extremely popular among unmarried girls of the area, and many informants described it as the highlight of the festival year. In preparation, elaboration, and expense, the festivities surrounding the celebration of the Double Seven in the delayed transfer marriage area appear to have been unsurpassed. Perhaps more than any other festival, the Double Seven provides the best example of how auxiliary forms of organization built on the relationships first established in the girls' house. In addition, an examination of the organization and interpretation of the Double Seven further illuminates the singular socialization experience of girls in this area.

The Double Seven festival, widely observed throughout Chinese society, celebrates the legend of the cowherd and the weaving maid, two celestial lovers embodied in the constellations Lyra and Aquila. On the basis of the available ethnographic reports, some fundamental features and a core account of this legend can tentatively be reconstructed. The celestial weaving maid was extremely diligent at her spinning and weaving, pleasing

*For further comment, see the footnote on p. 71.

her father, a celestial deity. After her father married her off to the cowherd, however, the weaving maid neglected her work. In anger, her father separated the couple. Since then, the weaving maid and the cowherd have been situated on opposite sides of the Milky Way and permitted to visit each other only once a year, on the night of the seventh day of the seventh month. According to ethnographic accounts, the Double Seven festival celebrates both the reunion of the celestial lovers and women's handicraft skills (for a standard account, see Yang 1945, 99–100; for an analysis of regional variation in the organization of the festival and interpretation of the legend, see Eberhard 1941 and Mann 1987).

Perhaps one reason for the central place of the Double Seven in the festival cycle of the Canton Delta is the special resonance between the legend of the separated celestial couple and the structure of delayed transfer marriage. The parallels between myth and marriage pattern are striking. As in Delta custom, the marital couple is separated by parental arrangement and allowed to visit only at specified times, ensuring that the celestial "bride-daughter" continues to work diligently. In the delayed transfer area, unmarried girls—the main celebrants of the Double Seven—celebrated the reunion of the celestial couple only secondarily. Instead, the primary focus of the festival altar and offerings were the weaving maid *and her six sisters*. In fact, the Double Seven was locally known among women as the festival of the Seven Sisters.* Girls in the delayed transfer marriage area worshiped the sisters with elaborate displays of their needle and handicraft skills.

An additional local twist given the legend was reported in 1880 by the wife of John Henry Gray.

A curious festival has also been held this week in honour of the Seven Sisters (goddesses), who are supposed by the Chinese to occupy a

---

*The Double Seven is also known as the Seven Sisters festival among Cantonese in Malaysia. For good accounts of this festival, see Wong 1967, 128–35; and Lo and Comber 1958, 31–33. Additional information on the Seven Sisters festival in the Canton Delta can be found in J. H. Gray 1878, 1:262; Mrs. Gray 1880, 281–85; Peplow and Barker 1931, 147–48; Gomes 1953; Burkhardt 1953–58, 1:32–35; and Ho 1958, 38, 141–42.

group of seven stars. It is said that one of these sisters made a clan-destine marriage with a cowherd occupying a planet on the other side of the Milky Way; and once a year the wife *is permitted by her sisters*, who were greatly incensed at her marriage, to cross the Milky Way to meet her husband. Women especially worship these Seven Sisters, and all influential families who are not in mourning . . . make grand prepara-tions for the observance of this ceremony. (Mrs. John Henry Gray 1880, 281–82; emphasis added)

The full import of the interpretation that a girl's "sisters" had an interest in controlling her marital behavior will become apparent in the discussion in the following chapters of radical practices within the delayed transfer marriage system.

The Seven Sisters festival was initiated by unmarried girls for an audience of families, neighbors, and fellow villagers. Accord-ing to informants, Seven Sisters "associations" consisted of from ten to more than twenty unmarried girls from one or more girls' houses. Some places had several Seven Sisters associations, but since membership required monthly contributions, not every girl belonged to one. Contributions ranged from twenty cents to as much as two or three dollars per month, which, as informants remarked, was a lot of money over the course of a year. Festival preparations, begun months in advance, entailed the produc-tion or purchase of items of furniture and clothing, which were used as offerings to the Seven Sisters and arranged on tables before a colorful altar of candles, incense, fruit, and flowers. Shoes, cosmetics, dresses, and tables and chairs were bought or made, often in miniature and always in multiples of seven, or one of every item for each of the seven sisters. (Sometimes a cos-tume was made for the cowherd and installed to one side of the altar. Mothers were said to worship the cowherd on behalf of their sons.) The elaborate preparations for the festival were or-ganized and often carried out in the evenings in the girls' house. For example, miniature shoes needed to be sewn and finely em-broidered, and small-scale furniture made and decorated with sesame seeds in intricate designs. Many kinds of fruits, sweets, and delicacies were purchased and prepared—seven dishes of each kind—and arranged for display on great tables. Some

Seven Sisters associations reportedly displayed as many as thirty tables, set out in a large courtyard, house, or ancestral hall. In some places, Seven Sisters associations competed to produce the most elaborate display. The members themselves made all the festival arrangements, in some places even hiring carpenters to build stages, musicians and players to perform, and cooks to prepare food to sell to the crowds. As one Sundak woman boasted, "The girls initiated everything themselves!" Informants reported that anyone could come; all the villagers were invited.

To those familiar with the secluded and confined lives of girls in other parts of China the activities of the members of these Seven Sisters associations must seem startling. In the organization and staging of the Seven Sisters festival, the "wish-fulfillment" banquet described earlier, and the Goddess of Mercy festival celebrated in some places, girls in the delayed transfer marriage area gained experience in making decisions and acting collectively, managing savings and budgeting funds, and participating in the public sphere to a degree unmatched in other parts of China. The special skills and expertise fostered in the festival associations and girls' houses, together with growing anti-marital biases and economic opportunities for young women in some places, were to prove important social preconditions for the rise of radical marriage-resistance practices in the late nineteenth and early twentieth centuries.

The end of a girl's participation in the Seven Sisters festival came after marriage, usually at pregnancy and just before her assumption of residence in her husband's home, but in some places after the first year of marriage. The occasion was in some villages marked by a banquet hosted by the departing member for the other girls (*chihsin*) in the Seven Sisters association. The cost of this ritual banquet was borne by the bridedaughter's husband's family, which provided funds to cover the purchase of roast pork, red buns and eggs, fruit, and delicacies for all members of the association. Thereafter, a woman celebrated the Seven Sisters festival only as part of the general audience.

THE WOMEN'S COMMUNITY

For a bridedaughter whose participation in a Seven Sisters association lasted for only the first year following her marriage, an
important focus of the women's community in her father's village came to an end. This did not mean, however, the end of a
bridedaughter's association with her unmarried female friends.
The continued association between a married woman and her
unmarried female friends was yet another distinctive feature
of the women's community in the delayed transfer marriage
area. Elsewhere in Chinese society, the immediate transfer of a
new wife to her husband's home on marriage more than likely
brought an abrupt end to contact between female friends. (In
point of fact, I know of no treatment of female friendship outside the Canton Delta in the ethnographic literature on traditional Chinese society.) In the delayed transfer marriage area,
however, continued natolocal residence for women for several
years after marriage provided the opportunity for continued
association.

One setting for contact between married and unmarried female friends was the girls' house. Although informants everywhere described girls' houses as intended for unmarried girls,
providing them with a gathering place and separate sleeping
accommodations, bridedaughters did continue to visit their
friends there. After all, as one informant observed, "All of them
had been friends for such a long time!" In some places bridedaughters reportedly even slept in the girls' house regularly, but
in most places bridedaughters lived at home with their parents
and only visited the girls' house. Some informants suggested
that unmarried girls did not like married women staying in the
girls' house. Others described bridedaughters as preferring to
sleep at home.

Although the practice of bridedaughters' sleeping in the
girls' house may even have varied house by house (space alone
would have been a consideration in some houses), the continuing close contact between bridedaughters and their unmarried

"sisters" had important implications for the women's community. Information about conjugal visits, restrictions in the husband's home, mothers-in-law, and sex was readily passed along by bridedaughters, thus shaping the perception of marriage among unmarried girls. In some places, as is shown in the following chapters, this information contributed to a vigorous antimarital bias among unmarried girls.

Another distinctive feature of the women's community in the delayed transfer marriage area was the significance of paternal aunts (father's sisters) in the socialization of girls and as role models. I know of no reference in the ethnographic literature on traditional Chinese society to the importance of the relationship between paternal aunts and their nieces. Indeed, this relationship seems a natural result of the delayed transfer marriage system itself. Postmarital intervals of natolocal residence for bridedaughters created a period of overlapping residence for lineage kinswomen of two generations. Many girls would have grown up in homes in which paternal aunts, especially father's younger sister(s), were still resident as bridedaughters.

According to informants' accounts, nieces looked up to their father's sister, who provided a natural role model as well as an introduction to a girls' house and a Seven Sisters association. Father's sisters, especially father's younger sisters, figure prominently in informants' sketches of marriage practices and economic strategies in the following chapters. As probably the most accessible representative of the older generation, father's younger sister was frequently mentioned in response to questions about the preceding generation or what I call the "mother's generation." In a typical example, a Sundak informant replying to a question about radical marriage-resistance practices (Was sworn spinsterhood practiced in your mother's generation?) responded that "one of father's younger sisters became a sworn spinster." In a more dramatic example, an informant described girls' houses in a town in Punyu.

Sih Kiuh was a big town that was divided into a lot of districts. According to the informant, there were girls' houses in every district. Usually at around 10 years of age girls started to group together in the girls' house. The informant's girls' house had two rooms, and eight to ten girls stayed there. The house itself was not specially built as a girls' house, but had been owned by her family for generations. Girls' houses were like that, she said. They were passed down from your father's father's sister to your own father's elder sister, then to your father's younger sister, then to you.

———

Father's sister, especially father's younger sister, thus occupied a special place as a senior female in father's family, a role model, a friend, and an advocate. In the delayed transfer marriage system—and in the following discussion of radical marriage-resistance practices—father's sisters emerge as central figures in the lives of their nieces.

3

Negotiating a
Compensation Marriage

Some bridedaughters refused ever to consummate their marriages. In a radical transaction that I call "compensation marriage," these bridedaughters renegotiated the terms of marriage with their husband's family. The often-lengthy negotiations were successfully concluded when the husband's family agreed to accept compensation from the bridedaughter and both parties settled on the amount to be paid. For the bridedaughter, payment of compensation radically extended the interval of spousal separation. Compensating bridedaughters returned to their husband's home only at old age or death. The husband's family used the compensation money to acquire a muijai who would marry in as a secondary wife. The arrangement of a compensation marriage was commonly referred to as "compensating and finding another wife" (*puih chin wan go yih naai*). Compensating bridedaughters were described as those who "didn't settle down in the husband's family" (*mh lohk ga*). The bridedaughter herself paid the compensation, out of money saved from her wages or borrowed from her "sisters." Her natal family did not contribute to the sum. Informants unanimously reported that compensation entailed one lump-sum payment—usually on the order of 300 dollars—and did not represent a continuing economic obligation on the part of the bridedaughter to her husband's family.

PRESERVING MARRIAGE AND ITS GUARANTEES

The heyday of compensation marriage lasted from 1890 to 1910. It was the first of several radical marriage-resistance practices to arise within the delayed transfer marriage area, under special circumstances and in some places. Because it was a radical practice, compensation marriage met with opposition from both the bridedaughter's natal family and that of her husband. But despite the radical nature of the practice, the payment of compensation was in fact intended to preserve a marriage, not to terminate it. A bridedaughter who paid compensation sought to maintain her marriage, although in altered form, because marriage guaranteed her future spiritual security. In this patrilineal society, it was through marriage, which provided a woman with an affiliation to a male descent line, that she acquired a place to die, an altar for her own ancestral tablet after her death, and a focus for her spirit in the afterlife.

Thus, for a woman, marriage was the path to spiritual security, what informants commonly called *muhn hau*. Although it translates as "entrance" or "doorway," the concept of spiritual security behind *muhn hau* seems best conveyed by the term *host*. Marriage secured a woman a host for her spirit and tablet. By compensating her husband, a bridedaughter sought to retain the host she acquired on marriage. For a woman contemplating anything other than a customary delayed transfer marriage, arranging a proper host for her spirit and tablet was a paramount concern. The elderly women who were my informants described how even as girls they had had this concern foremost in their minds as they plotted and planned alternative marriage strategies.

Compensation made possible a prolonged delay in the completion of the marriage process for the bridedaughter. In effect, the bridedaughter contracted out to a secondary wife certain claims and obligations associated with the status of wife that she herself had renounced, while retaining others, the most important of which was her claim to a place in the husband's home for her tablet. Some places had a saying that in compensation marriage, "one wife substitutes for the other." This seemingly straightforward substitution of a secondary wife for a primary wife was in fact not easily arranged. As a radical departure from traditional delayed transfer marriage, the practice of compensation marriage was hedged with proscriptions. Successfully arranging a compensation marriage, however, safeguarded a young woman's future in a way that simple desertion could not.

The 74-year-old informant lived on the edge of Siu Laahm in Jungsaan in a multi-surname settlement, Waih Hau. This area had a mixed economy, based on fishing, the cultivation of rice and mulberry trees, and silkworm rearing. Although silk cocoons were primarily exported to Sundak for reeling in the big steam filatures, some silk was reeled in Waih Hau, at home by hand. When the mulberry leaf and cocoon harvests were complete in her own family, a girl in Waih Hau could earn wages harvesting and reeling for other families in the village.

In Waih Hau, women married with delayed transfer and settled with their husband only after several years of marriage, when their husband's family urged them to come or their own family urged them to go. According to the informant, there were few compensating bridedaughters in her own generation, but the practice had been more popular in the preceding generation. There was no "early" compensation in Waih Hau, only "late" compensation, paid after several years of marriage before a bridedaughter settled in her husband's home [see below for further discussion of early and late compensation]. The compensating bridedaughter made one payment to her husband's family. She gave them money that she herself had saved from her earnings, because her parents wouldn't provide her with funds for compensation. If a bridedaughter didn't want to return to her husband and had no money with which to compensate his family, her only recourse was to run away. But running away without paying compensation meant that her tablet could not be placed in her husband's home. By contrast, a bridedaughter who paid compensation could return to her husband's home to die and have her tablet placed there after death.

For the compensating bridedaughter, postponement of her assumption of the status of wife meant that for perhaps twenty years she occupied a somewhat anomalous position, neither completely inside nor completely outside a customary delayed transfer marriage. A compensating bridedaughter in effect held the status of non-customary bridedaughter, to which no claims and obligations were ascribed. Each bridedaughter individually negotiated her relationship with her own and her husband's family. There was, therefore, great variation in the arrangement and practice of compensation marriage, as illustrated in the accounts below. In spite of this variation, however, informants' accounts convey the general sense that compensation marriage was never socially endorsed and was only tolerated in some places and disallowed in many more.

THE SOCIAL CONTEXT

The temporal and spatial distributions of compensation marriage and other marriage-resistance practices are analyzed in Chapters 6–8 below. A few temporal and spatial considerations are, however, basic to a description of this form of marriage resistance. First, compensation marriage was found only within the delayed transfer marriage area. Compensation marriage did not—and logically could not—occur within major-marriage areas since it entailed the extension of a preexisting, customary period of postmarital separation that was a feature exclusive to delayed transfer marriage. It is clear from the written record, examined in Chapter 6, that compensation marriage has not usually been perceived as a radical variant of the customary delayed transfer form of marriage. In fact, as equally aberrant practices by the standards of the major-marriage system, delayed transfer marriage and compensation marriage have frequently been confused and conflated in accounts by outsiders, both Westerners and Chinese from other parts of China. Wives living apart from husbands were perceived, or at the very least portrayed, as wives who refused to live with their husbands.

Second, within the delayed transfer marriage area, compensation marriage occurred only in places offering wage work for bridedaughters, a source of compensation funds. The amount of compensation was intended to cover the entire cost of the secondary marriage. As one informant said, "When you told the husband's family that you wanted to compensate, you had to assure them that they didn't need to spend even one penny on the second marriage!" In fact, a bridedaughter had no hope of negotiating a compensation marriage without access to about 300 dollars, the most frequently quoted compensation figure. (This is also the figure usually quoted for bridewealth, but the payment of compensation was not technically the return of the bridewealth. Bridewealth and dowry were the mark of a valid primary marriage, which compensating bridedaughters sought to preserve.)

Because 300 dollars was a significant sum, bridedaughters intent on arranging compensation marriages were dependent on employment generating substantial wages. The most commonly cited sources for compensation funds were silk reeling and, later, domestic service, especially in Canton and Hong Kong. Silk reeling, which figures significantly in my analysis of the rise of the marriage-resistance practices in Chapter 8, is the critical role in silk production in which the silk fiber is unwound from the cocoon. A labor-intensive, highly skilled job, silk reeling was performed in the Canton Delta by women only. For a silk reeler, 300 dollars represented about two years' wages in a silk factory, or "filature." Informants frequently spoke of compensating bridedaughters as synonymous with silk reelers: "Compensation money was from a woman's own earnings as a silk reeler." "Silk reelers didn't want to settle with their husbands." In fact, it was usually as reelers in silk centers, or "spinners" as they were sometimes called, that compensating bridedaughters were most visible to outsiders. In the late 1920's, Agnes Smedley, the celebrated American journalist, toured the Canton Delta silk area. She describes her official escort's reaction to silk reelers, a reaction toward delayed transfer marriage and marriage-resistance practices typical of both Western and Chinese outsiders:

When he spoke of the silk peasants or the girl filature workers, hostility and contempt crept into his voice. His particular hatred seemed to be the thousands of women spinners, and only with difficulty could I learn why. He told me that the women were notorious throughout China as lesbians. They refused to marry, and if their families forced them, they merely bribed their husbands with a part of their wages and induced them to take concubines. (Smedley 1943, 87)

The mechanization of silk reeling in the late nineteenth century and subsequent employment of women in steam-powered filatures was a critical factor in the rise of compensation marriage and the other marriage-resistance practices. However, the efflorescence of compensation marriage was not simply a function of economic opportunity for bridedaughters. Another important factor was the growth of an anti-marital bias among young women during the nineteenth century, primarily in sericultural villages. The various marriage-resistance practices in fact fall into a temporal sequence. The heyday of compensation marriage preceded the rise of sworn spinsterhood. This temporal relationship, analyzed in Chapter 7, is suggested by the following accounts.

A 75-year-old Sundak informant from Gam Juk Yauh Taan, near the silk center of Daaih Leuhng, reported that in her generation women either married in the customary fashion with delayed transfer or became sworn spinsters. How-

ever, in the preceding generation, some women had practiced compensation marriage, settling in their husband's
family only after many years. In those cases, compensation
money was used to buy a secondary wife for the husband.
The informant cited as an example her father's elder brother's
wife, who had compensated and returned to her husband's
home to die twenty years later.

A 59-year-old informant was from a small single-surname
village in the cluster of villages that make up Gong Meih in
Sundak. In her village, rice fields were situated near hilly
areas, but the village economy primarily depended on the
cultivation of mulberry groves and silkworm rearing. Girls
earned wages working for other families, harvesting mulberry leaves, raising silkworms, reeling silk, and doing farm
chores. In the informant's own generation, a lot of women
left the village as sworn spinsters to find work in other villages, some even migrating to Hong Kong. Those women
who stayed in the village married in the customary fashion
with delayed transfer. Girls were usually engaged at 17 or 18
and married one or two years later. There were no compensating bridedaughters in the informant's own generation, but
there had been in her mother's generation. (Her mother was
then 80 years old.) The informant cited as an example of
a compensating bridedaughter her own "grandmother," a
woman with bound feet, who was her grandfather's first
wife. "Grandmother" didn't want to live with her husband
and arranged to pay compensation. The informant said that
her real grandmother was a secondary wife, formerly a muijai, who had been purchased with the compensation money.

Before the heyday of compensation marriage in the late nineteenth century, the growing anti-marital bias found expression
in female suicide among young women who were determined
to remain unwed or to avoid settling with their husband and
who had no recourse to marriage alternatives. Early- and mid-
nineteenth century documents record incidents of both individ-

ual and "collective" suicide, which I consider in my analysis of anti-marital bias in Chapter 7. At this juncture, one documented case of an individual suicide will serve as an example of the strength of the local sentiment against marriage and the extremes to which some girls were willing to go to avoid it. In addition, this case illustrates the way in which suicides in this area conformed to the distinctive structure of delayed transfer marriages. Taken from the work of John Henry Gray, the account concerns the fate of a bridedaughter during a conjugal visit to her husband's home in Punyu county.

I may narrate the sad sequel of the marriage of a youth with whom I was well acquainted. This youth, Ng Acheong by name, a native of a village situated at the base of the Lin-fa Hills, in the vicinity of the Bogue Forts, where this custom [delayed transfer marriage] is strictly practised, was called upon during the month immediately following his marriage to leave the provincial capital where his duties were, on a short visit of ceremony to his parents, who were expecting to be honoured by the presence of his bride, their daughter-in-law.

The bride was the first to arrive. On the morning following her arrival, however, it was discovered that during the night she had committed suicide by taking poison. It appeared she had carefully concealed the poison—which was a root called Woo-Mun-Kaong by the Chinese—in her clothing previous to the departure from her father's house. A few hours after this discovery the bride-groom arrived, only to receive the intelligence of the suicide of his bride. This singular and foolish custom also prevails in the county of Shun-tuk [Sundak], which is one of the political divisions of the province of Kwang-tung. With the view of suppressing it, the magistrates of the district in question not unfrequently issue proclamations calling upon parents to compel their daughters to reside at once with their husbands. (Gray 1878, 1:208)

It was common practice throughout much of the delayed transfer marriage area for parents to conceal from their daughters the arrangement of their marriage. Ho It Chong, a sociologist who interviewed Delta immigrants in Singapore, gives the following account of this practice:

Yin Tse and three other amahs [domestic servants] said they had known a few of their village "sisters" who, to avoid marriage, had resorted to suicide on learning that they had been betrothed to be married. For this reason parents of marriageable daughters kept their betrothal secret from their daughters until the last few days before the actual marriage day and were strict to see that their daughters remain in the house after they had betrothed them for marriage. It was also for this reason that custom [forbade] any person to break the news to the girl concerned. (Ho 1958, 134)

My informants did not report suicide as a primary motivation in their own generation for the concealment of marriage arrangements. However, they did say that parents were afraid their daughters would run away if they learned marriage was imminent. Whatever the origin of the practice of concealing marriage arrangements, young women came to depend on the watchful eyes of their "sisters" to learn that marriage negotiations were under way. As mentioned above, one consuming topic of conversation in the girls' house was which family was arranging a marriage. Informants said that one sure sign of an impending match was a young woman's discovery that a group of men was watching her closely on the street. There were other signs: "You could tell when your parents had arranged a marriage for you," recounted one informant, "because the house looked especially clean and neat, and suddenly there were gifts you had never seen before. But you just pretended nothing had happened and continued to go out as usual."

Another informant gave a comparative account of the arrangement of marriage inside and outside the delayed transfer marriage area:

The informant was from a Naahmhoi village, one of a cluster of more than ten villages of eight surnames surrounding the market town of Gam Jiu. She reported that in every village in Gam Jiu, women on marriage at once settled down with their husbands [*jikhaak lohk ga*]. Girls were engaged around 14 or 15 years of age, and married at 17 or 18. According to the informant, it wasn't popular for girls in Gam Jiu to say they didn't want to marry. She explained that girls had no jobs for which they were paid. Gam Jiu was in a rice-producing area and girls weren't hired as farm laborers. They married, raised children, and did chores in their husband's home. But in Sundak, she said, girls refused to do these things. In Gam Jiu, girls had to depend on their parents before marriage and on their husband after marriage. All girls married, and Gam Jiu parents told their daughters when marriage was arranged. The informant said it wasn't like in Sundak, where parents had to conceal arrangements from their daughters—even hiding the engagement cakes!

There were several stages to the arrangement of delayed transfer marriages. The first stage was the matching of the horoscopes of the prospective bride and groom. This was accomplished through the services of a matchmaker and was called *hoi nihn saang*. If no inauspicious event occurred during the time the horoscopes were being matched and both families wished to proceed with the marriage, a date was chosen for the visit of the groom's father to the bride's family to negotiate terms.

On the day of the visit, it was arranged that the bride-to-be was absent from home, staying with friends or family. Subjects for negotiation that day included the size and content of the bridewealth and dowry and the arrangement and timing of conjugal visits. When the two families reached an agreement, the match was formally sealed with a token gift of cakes sent by the groom's family to the bride's, typically presented in two large red boxes. Called *gwo mahn dihng*, this transaction was also concealed from the bride. It was on the occasion of *gwo mahn dihng*, however, that a bride's "sisters" in the girls' house hoped to learn of the proceedings and communicate them to the bride.

The next stage in the arrangement of marriage was the exchange of the bridewealth and dowry, or *gwo daaih laih*. Not uncommonly, parents also succeeded in keeping news of the marriage arrangements secret from the bride until after the delivery of the bridewealth to the bride's home. Informants described bridewealth as typically consisting of roast pig, noodles, cakes, and at least 300 dollars in silver.

A married informant from Naahmhoi explained that a girl was usually sent from home on a one- or two-day visit to another village at the time the bridewealth was exchanged. On the arranged day, the groom's family set two special cakes before a statue of the Buddha. One of these cakes was then eaten by the groom and the other sent along with the bridewealth to the bride's home. On her return home, the bride was tricked into eating this cake, which meant that she and her husband would have a good relationship. An old woman, distinguished for having raised many children, then pushed the bride on the back, announcing her betrothal. At this news most girls cried!

Dowry, which accompanied the bride to the groom's home on the wedding day, typically included a bridal bed quilt, tables, chairs, clothes in red boxes, a basin, a tea pot and other cooking pots, ritual money, and a basket of food. Sometimes a shop sign was added to the above inventory, indicating that the bride's family was sufficiently wealthy to include, for instance, a pawn shop as part of the dowry.

Informants reported that it was customary for the engaged girl to be confined at home for several days before her marriage and not allowed to go out as had been her habit. Although she could not go to the girls' house, her "sisters" joined her at home, staying with her and lamenting her fate.

NEGOTIATING STRATEGIES

Those bridedaughters intent on practicing compensation marriage usually initiated the process by running away, often to a silk center. A bridedaughter ran away on her wedding day or later during a conjugal visit, individual circumstances and opportunity determining the most expedient strategy. Runaway bridedaughters typically spent a few years working and saving before beginning negotiations with the husband's family. Then the bridedaughter either contacted the husband's family herself or engaged a go-between. Once begun, the negotiations were sometimes lengthy affairs. If successful, the husband's family agreed to accept compensation, thereby preserving the marriage and guaranteeing the bridedaughter's claim to die in the husband's home, as well as a place there for her spirit and tablet. Some informants claimed that a compensating bridedaughter could visit her husband's home any time she liked, although obligatory visits ceased with compensation. Other informants spoke of strained relations with the husband's family, saying that some compensating bridedaughters did not want to return, even to die.

The following account illustrates a common compensation strategy.

The informant, a 71-year-old woman from Mah Chyun in Sundak, arranged a compensation marriage for herself. At the time of *gwo mahn dihng*, when the arrangement of the marriage was formalized, the informant's "sisters" managed to let her know of the impending match. The informant then ran away to Hong Kong, where she worked for five or six years before returning to talk to her husband's family about compensation. Agreement was reached, and the informant paid 300 dollars in compensation. She explained that her mother didn't object to her decision to compensate because she was an only daughter.

Some brides managed to run away on the very day of marriage, some even from the bridal sedan chair. Others tried to run away as soon as possible after the worship of the ancestors and gods that constituted the marriage ritual.

According to a Punyu informant, a friend had run away to Canton on the very day she married by hiding for a while in an empty grave. From Canton she went to Japan, where she worked as a domestic servant. After ten years, she wrote to her brothers to tell her husband to find another wife with the money she would send. The secondary wife eventually had a son, who, when grown, asked his "first mother" to return for his marriage.

———

One singular case of compensation entailed a runaway husband instead of the usual runaway bridedaughter.

———

An informant from Sin Chung in Sundak recounted the experience of her father's younger sister. On the evening of her marriage, this aunt deliberately broke custom in the bedroom by speaking first, asking her husband, "Does your family manage a bank?" Her husband was so alarmed at his new bride's breach of custom that he fled the room and ran away to a secondary wife. The bridedaughter returned home. She was later invited by her mother-in-law to visit, but her husband refused to have anything to do with her. The husband's family therefore agreed to accept compensation from the bridedaughter, who afterward continued to live at home and reel silk.

———

The transaction itself, the actual payment of compensation by the bridedaughter to the husband's family, was often hedged with proscriptions. In some places the payment was felt to be so irregular and even polluting that it was not permitted to take place on family land or within village boundaries (which in the case of single-surname villages were often one and the same). So great was the risk of pollution that some believed grass would not grow on the spot where compensation had been transacted.*

———

An 81-year-old informant from Jung Chyun in Punyu explained that in order to arrange a compensation marriage, a

———

*In Taiwan, divorce was similarly perceived as polluting. "Divorce was no more acceptable in Hai-shan than on the China mainland. Indeed, people in Hai-shan appear to have regarded divorce as an abnormal, even polluting, act. No sooner was a document declaring divorce signed than it was partially burned to dispel baneful influences, and immediately after, the leftover ink was thrown away, preferably in some isolated spot away from human habitation. One old man told us that 'the grass withers around the place where the ink is thrown'" (A. Wolf and Huang 1980, 178).

woman had to run away first, returning later to compensate. However, a bridedaughter was not allowed to compensate within village boundaries. Instead, she had to take the money outside the village before giving it to a representative of the husband's family. According to the informant, a witness was always present when compensation was paid.

The following case provides another example of constraints on the practice of compensation. In this instance, the account is set within fuller description of the local economy and marriage practices.

The 78-year-old informant was from Wohng Gok, a rice-growing village in Punyu. Few men left the village to seek work elsewhere. Girls did farm work, cutting grass and harvesting rice, and could earn wages doing this for other families. Delayed transfer marriage was practiced in Wohng Gok, and bridedaughters settled with their husbands when they became pregnant. Intervals were usually seven to eight years, or four to five if the bridedaughter became pregnant sooner. There were only three compensating wives in the informant's generation. The informant said families in Wohng Gok didn't allow compensation and wouldn't accept it. Bridedaughters had to run away to force families to permit compensation. Compensation always occurred several years after marriage. Usually, the bridedaughter sent an old woman or her "sisters" to pay compensation, but compensation could not be transacted in the village itself. The bridedaughter's representatives had to go beyond the village to a remote place to compensate—like to the hills or some other unsettled place. The bridedaughter made one lump-sum payment from her own earnings.

Some bridedaughters arranged to deliver the compensation money directly to their mothers-in-law. An informant from Sin Chung in Sundak knew a woman who put her compensation money in a three-tiered black basket decorated with a gold design and took it herself to her mother-in-law. Compensation had been arranged through an old woman, known to the bride-daughter's mother. Another Sundak informant described how in her village, Chahn Chyun, one woman arranged her hair in a bun, dressed like a bride, and, accompanied by her "sisters," took the basket containing the compensation money directly to her mother-in-law.

In some cases, instead of making a payment, a compensating bridedaughter located and acquired a secondary wife for her husband. In other cases, the husband's family selected a second-ary wife, and the compensating bridedaughter covered the ex-pense. In this case, as one compensating bridedaughter put it, "You had to pay for every cent that was spent on soy sauce!" However acquired, the secondary wife married into the family according to a standard ritual. As one Sundak informant, from Mahk Chyun, described it: "After worshiping the groom's an-cestors, a secondary wife went to the home of the first wife to serve tea and then returned to the groom's home to serve tea to her parents-in-law." By the act of serving tea to the first wife, a secondary wife acknowledged her inferior status not only as a wife but, as explained below, as a mother, too.

Some women initiated compensation negotiations after par-ticipating for several years in married life in the customary man-ner. This category of compensating bridedaughters included those who on marriage had not originally planned to compen-sate. According to informants, this was a minority group, and most bridedaughters who compensated were decided on that course of action from the start.

An informant from Lahk Lauh in Sundak described how her elder sister eventually came to compensate her husband's family. This sister had been married for some time and had visited her husband in the customary "back-and-forth" man-ner [*loihloih wohngwohng*]. However, even after several years of visiting, she was still unable to feel comfortable with her husband and his family. She therefore took the opportunity while on a conjugal visit to run away to Hong Kong, where she found work as a domestic servant. When she eventually returned home, her husband came to negotiate and agreed to accept compensation.

———

Informants reported that after several years of married life, some bridedaughters simply refused any further invitations to visit their husband's family. One informant described how she ran away and hid in a neighbor's house every time her husband's family sent someone to invite her for a visit. This refusal to meet a basic obligation of customary marriage provoked a crisis that set negotiations in motion. Some bridedaughters, rather than refusing to visit outright, reportedly indulged in spiteful behavior during conjugal visits, aimed at persuading resistant parents-in-law to accept compensation. Such bridedaughters might, when repeatedly urged to assume cooking chores on visits, respond by cooking up all the rice in the house, using up all the cooking oil, or burning up all the firewood. Sometimes mothers-in-law, anxious for grandchildren and growing impatient with daughters-in-law who balked at staying with their husbands, pressed their daughters-in-law to compensate. Many conflicts over "cooking" and "visiting" were doubtless at heart conflicts over fertility.

A few informants mentioned that a village known for its large number of compensating bridedaughters might be passed over by families in search of brides for their sons.

———

A 75-year-old informant from a sericultural village near Gau Gong in Naahmhoi reported that few bridedaughters had compensated in her own generation, but that the practice had been more popular in the preceding generation. She said that her father had taken a bride from the distant town of Faht Saan in order to avoid marrying a woman who might later compensate.

———

In one case reported by a compensating bridedaughter, an 83-year-old woman from Sam Kiuh in Punyu county, the husband was so fearful that any other wife would also want to arrange for compensation that he decided not to marry again and emigrated overseas instead.

One of the factors cited earlier as probably affecting the length of the period of separation in delayed transfer marriages was the relative power of the bridedaughter's and husband's families and the power relations between the lineages to which those families belonged. These relations must also have figured significantly in the arrangement of compensation marriages. The relative power and status of the husband's family and lineage would surely have been factors in determining whether his family would agree to accept compensation. Was it the case that the greater the power and status differential between the two families, the less likely the husband's family was to accept compensation? Because my research is based on retrospective interviews with Canton Delta emigrants, I do not have the data to address this question effectively. Nevertheless, that family power and status did influence the arrangement of compensation marriages is suggested by informants' accounts. A few informants reported that compensation was accepted only when the husband's family was poor. As one informant put it, "Those families with money could buy their own secondary wives!" One account is especially suggestive of the role of power and status in the arrangement of compensation marriage.

_____

The 73-year-old informant said that in her village, a single-surname village in Gong Meih in Sundak county, if a girl really didn't want to marry, she could arrange to marry a man from a poor family who couldn't afford to marry. She gave him money to buy a secondary wife, and in return, she acquired the right as first wife to go to his home to die. The informant reported that although there were still cases of compensation marriage in her own generation, there had been many more cases in her grandmother's generation. She knew that one of her own "grandmothers," a fourth wife in a wealthy family, had wanted to pay compensation to her grandfather, but he had refused to accept it. He wanted her to stay with him. So her "grandmother" had committed suicide by drowning herself.

EARLY VERSUS LATE COMPENSATION

In customary delayed transfer marriages, pregnancy and childbearing were delayed. In compensation marriages, the claims and obligations defining marriage were renegotiated, and the secondary wife assumed the responsibility of childbearing. Because compensation could not be arranged after the birth of a baby, bridedaughters determined to arrange compensation marriages were equally determined to avoid pregnancy, which would trigger the transition in status to wife and the assumption of permanent virilocal residence. Bridedaughters intent on avoiding childbearing, as opposed to merely delaying it in the customary manner, resorted to the surest means to prevent pregnancy, non-consummation of the marriage. One means of ensuring this is described by Marjorie Topley: "[Some] women took herbal medicines to suppress micturition and set off for their wedding ceremonies with strips of cloth wrapped mummy fashion under their bridal gown to prevent consummation" (1975, 67).

According to my own informants, body-wrapping was not a practice generally current in the generation of informants aged 60 to 85, who were born between 1895 and 1920. Some had heard of body-wrapping from women of an older generation (one Naahmhoi informant reported, "I heard father's elder sisters talk about it"). Attributable to the same general period as the heyday of compensation marriage (1890–1910), body-wrapping was probably one of the extreme measures employed by bridedaughters intent on arranging compensation marriages.

A 64-year-old informant from the rich silk center of Yuhng Keih in Sundak gave one account of the practice of body-wrapping. She said that in Yuhng Keih compensation marriages had been more common in the preceding generation.

Some of her own paternal great-aunts had been compensating wives. Although body-wrapping had not been practiced in her own generation, she had heard how at one time women had been wrapped and stitched into their undergarments "just like dumplings." They were given pills to prevent urination, and on their return from conjugal visits, their "sisters" had checked to see that the seam was intact. The informant said she had heard her great-aunts tell how once a knife was discovered tucked into the cloth wrapping and that as a result the practice of body-wrapping was forbidden.

The struggle to maintain childlessness before compensation could be arranged was obviated by the practice of "immediate" or early compensation (*jikhaak puih chin*). This form of compensation was much less widespread over the delayed transfer marriage area than the "late" form (compensation arranged after several years of marriage). Early compensation was an even more radical departure from customary delayed transfer marriage than was late compensation. By early compensation, parents and future in-laws permitted compensation before marriage. One Naahmhoi informant explained that compensation could be arranged before marriage *if* a girl declared her desire to compensate at the time of *gwo mahn dihng* and *if* her parents weren't conservative. Of course, in addition to parental consent, early compensation required that a woman have immediate access to sufficient funds. Thus, this form of compensation marriage, dependent on both a more liberal climate and lucrative employment, occurred primarily in silk centers.

In early compensation, a muijai to act as secondary wife was acquired with the compensation money before the first bride's marriage. Then, in an extraordinary ceremony, both brides married on the same day. Two sedan chairs proceeded to the groom's house, the red one conveying the compensating first bride, the green one the secondary bride. This variation of compensation marriage was most commonly referred to as "passing through the doorway together" (*yatchai gwo muhn*).

Informants reported that in cases of early compensation no dowry or only a token dowry was exchanged. Of course, for girls permitted to arrange early compensation at the time of *gwo mahn dihng*, no dowry would have as yet been paid. In a case described below of a girl who arranged for early compensation after the bridewealth and dowry had been exchanged, the dowry was returned. Undoubtedly various terms were negotiated to suit individual circumstances. In cases of late compensation, however, dowry was reportedly not returned. According to informants, the dowry in cases of late compensation was used by the secondary wife. One Punyu informant explained that "dowry was paid because parents didn't know their daughter would compensate." Other informants felt that in cases of late compensation the husband's family's retention of the dowry helped ensure that the bridedaughter would be allowed to return there to die.

The marriage ritual in cases of early compensation reflected the differential status of the two brides. The compensating first bride bowed to the ancestors and served tea to her parents-in-law. She was in turn served tea by the secondary bride, who addressed her as "first wife." After the ritual, the secondary bride spent the night with their husband, immediately assuming the role of wife. The compensating first bride, by contrast, immediately departed for home to begin her tenure as bridedaughter, which might last as long as twenty years or more.

———

A Sundak informant recounted the case of her cousin, her mother's brother's elder daughter. Her marriage had been arranged, and the dowry and bridewealth had been exchanged. At the last minute, however, her cousin managed to arrange for a compensation marriage and paid 300 dollars before the wedding. A muijai to act as secondary wife was found, and both first and secondary brides then married on the same day [*yatchai gwo muhn*]. After the wedding, her cousin did not stay overnight but immediately returned home. In this case, the bridedaughter's parents received the dowry back, but the bridewealth was not returned.

———

The compensating bridedaughter retained her claim to the status of first wife even while contracting out to the secondary wife most of the customary claims and obligations associated with the status of wife. In like manner, the compensating bridedaughter retained her claim to the status of "first mother" even though the children were born to the secondary wife. To the children of the secondary wife, the compensating bridedaughter was "first wife" and was called "big mother" (*daaih ma*). To her own children, the secondary wife was known as "little mother" (*sai ma*).

Some compensating bridedaughters reportedly visited their "children" on occasion, taking them gifts of clothes and jewelry. Others assumed more formal roles as children were born to the secondary wife, for instance, covering the expense of the ritual customarily performed one month after birth. Sons of the secondary wife, when old enough, reportedly paid their respects to their first mother. And when a son or daughter married, tea was served to the compensating bridedaughter, who as first mother took ritual precedence over the biological mother.

PATTERNS OF BEHAVIOR

In effect, compensation marriage radically extended the traditional delayed transfer marriage process. Through the renegotiation of the terms of marriage and the payment of compensation, marriage was preserved, and a bridedaughter's obligations to the husband's family were redefined. These altered claims and obligations were manifest in changed patterns of residence, production, consumption, and sexual behavior that varied in response to individual factors and local constraints. The pattern of sexual behavior appeared to be the most consistent one among compensating bridedaughters. Because compensation had to be negotiated before pregnancy and the assumption of virilocal residence, bridedaughters strove to prevent consummation of the marriage. Abdication of childbearing, however, did not mean that a compensating bridedaughter forfeited parenthood. Secondary wives provided children to compensating bridedaughters as well as to their husband. The sons of secondary wives were responsible for attending to the tablets of deceased first mothers. In addition, a consistent pattern of production characterized the behavior of compensating bridedaughters. Informants reported that a compensating bridedaughter bore no economic obligation to her affines after the lump-sum payment of compensation. The benefits of a compensating bridedaughter's labor were enjoyed by the bridedaughter herself, often by her natal family, and also, if she chose, by the children of the secondary wife.

Perhaps the most variable feature of compensation marriage, in addition to the actual strategies employed to achieve it, was the pattern of residence. Residence reflected different individual and local constraints on the practice of compensation marriage. In some cases bridedaughters continued to reside natolocally until they eventually assumed virilocal residence. In cases of continued natolocal residence, bridedaughters also remained producers and consumers in their natal families. However, the economic benefit to natal families was not the sole factor influencing the residence of compensating bridedaughters. In some places, compensating bridedaughters were reportedly prohibited from living at home if a sister-in-law was already in residence. In other places, where there was strong local sentiment against the practice of compensation marriage, natolocal residence was not an option. Employment was still another constraint on natolocal residence. Compensating bridedaughters often migrated beyond natal villages to secure the wage-generating employment on which their livelihood and compensation depended.

The pattern of residence for compensating bridedaughters was obviously problematic. As detailed in the discussion in the next two chapters on sworn spinsterhood and bride-initiated spirit marriage, residence was a major constraint on all forms of marriage resistance.

4

Becoming a Sworn Spinster

Another marriage-resistance practice in the delayed transfer marriage area was sworn spinsterhood. Sworn spinsterhood was not simply a status ascribed to women who remained unmarried, but one achieved through a special ritual. Central to that ritual was a hairdressing ceremony, and sworn spinsters were known as those who had combed up their own hair (*jihso neuih*, or simply *sohei*). Sworn spinsters chose spinsterhood over marriage with the endorsement of their natal family in some cases and over family objections in others. In the early twentieth century, sworn spinsterhood offered Canton Delta women the ultimate independent way of life. Many of my informants were themselves spinsters or had sisters or paternal aunts who were spinsters.

Typically self-supporting, spinsters depended on wage-generating employment. The search for a livelihood and for escape from local constraints on the practice of spinsterhood frequently propelled spinsters toward distant and lucrative employment in silk and service centers. Spinsterhood was for many spinsters and their natal family a sojourning strategy, in which spinster daughters, profitably employed beyond natal villages, sent remittances home to their family.

Although the motivations for choosing spinsterhood over marriage varied, two basic sentiments can be discerned: a rejection of the claims and obligations of marriage and an affirmation of the spinster life-style. Informants explained their choice of spinsterhood by saying they were afraid of marriage or mothers-in-law, they wanted to be independent and earn their own living, they did not want a husband or were afraid a husband would take more than one wife, they were afraid of childbirth or did not know how to care for children, they desired to be their own person and do as they pleased, or they wanted to avoid the "bother" of marriage.*

RITUALS, FAMILY RELATIONS, AND STATUS

As with compensation marriage, no claims and obligations were ascribed to sworn spinsterhood; each spinster individually negotiated relations with her natal family. The practice of spinsterhood varied considerably, reflecting different individual circumstances and local constraints. In an effort to describe the variable arrangements that characterized this non-customary status, informants frequently made analogies with more customary statuses. Thus, the status of spinsterhood was described as "like marriage." Spinster daughters, though unmarried, were described as "like married daughters" in some respects, yet were treated like unmarried daughters in others. In still other respects, spinsters were described by informants as like sons. As we shall see, there was some truth in all these comparisons.

*Motivations for becoming a spinster are also considered in Ho 1958, 23–30; Topley 1975, 79–80; Sankar 1978, 84–114; Greenway 1987; and Jaschok 1984, 1987, 266–67. Although my own research did not specifically address the issue of lesbianism, it suggests that this was not a primary reason for the popularity of sworn spinsterhood (see also Chapter 2). This conclusion is supported by Greenway 1987, 153; and Jaschok 1987, 275; but see also Sankar 1985 for a discussion of one lesbian relationship between two sworn spinsters.

Traditionally, women achieved adulthood only upon marriage. Informants described the spinster ritual as resembling marriage in that it initiated a woman into adulthood. As one Sundak informant recalled, spinsterhood was "like marriage" in that spinsters were treated as adults and shown respect. As a sign of this respect, for example, spinsters were served tea at the weddings of their younger brothers and sisters.

Ideally, where there were few constraints on the practice of spinsterhood, the spinster ritual was conducted at home before the domestic ancestors and gods. The central features of the spinster ceremony were the hairdressing ritual, a vow of celibacy, and worship of the domestic ancestors and gods. As in the marriage ceremony, the hairdressing ritual symbolized the assumption of a new status. According to informants, the spinster hairdressing ritual entailed combing a girl's bangs back from her face and fixing her hair into a bun. The spinster's bun was described as a simple one with plain pins, in contrast to the more elaborate buns with colorful pins that could be worn by married women. As with the hairdressing ritual for brides at marriage, the hairdressing ritual for sworn spinsters was always performed by a woman of a different surname. Although arranging the bun was a central feature of the spinster ritual, wearing a bun was not essential to spinster identity, and spinsters customarily wore their hair tied back in a single braid. Similarly, while spinsters donned skirts for the spinster ritual, they continued to use pants for everyday wear.

In the marriage ritual, a bride worshiped before her husband's ancestors, marking her new affiliation with her husband's descent line. Significantly, in the spinster ritual, a woman worshiped before the domestic ancestors of her natal family, that is, the immediate ancestors in her father's descent line. In a sense, worshiping before her father's ancestors extended a spinster's affiliation with that line. This affiliation was more extensive in some places than in others, especially where the metaphor of spinsters as sons was most complete.

The affiliation of spinster daughters with father's descent line was also expressed in some places in another modified nuptial ritual. A bride in some villages in the delayed transfer marriage area traditionally sewed pants for the men in her new husband's immediate family, including her husband, his younger and elder brothers, and his father. A spinster, however, sewed pants for the men in her own father's family, including her father and her younger and elder brothers.

Where constraints were few and families endorsed their daughters' decisions to become spinsters, the spinster ritual was celebrated in the home and followed by a banquet for family and friends. In these places, a daughter simply declared, before her marriage was arranged, her desire to remain unwed and become a spinster. Generally, there were fewer constraints on spinsterhood in towns and prosperous villages, and it was there that spinsters were found in greatest numbers. As one Sundak informant observed of her own county, "The main towns of Sundak were not conservative, and many spinsters lived in those places." Although there were spinsters in small villages, too, local constraints and conservatism caused many village spinsters to migrate to less restrictive settings.

Some villages forbade the practice of spinsterhood outright, and would-be spinsters had to run away. An informant from a single-surname village in Gong Meih in Sundak reported that any village girl who wanted to become a spinster had no choice but to run away. She knew she had to run when she learned that her parents were preparing to exchange her horoscope (*hoi nihn saang*) with a prospective husband.

An informant from Siu Laahm in Jungsaan, where parents did not readily endorse spinsterhood for their daughters, describes the strategy she employed to become a spinster:

The third daughter in a family of five daughters and two sons, the informant was the only spinster in her family and considers herself "naughty." She explained that since marriage was a lot of trouble, "capable" girls ran away to Hong Kong to work as domestic servants and become spinsters. She said that she was afraid of marriage, but her parents would not allow her to become a spinster. According to the informant, parents in Siu Laahm did not want their daughters to become spinsters. Therefore, girls never told their parents of their desire to become spinsters, but went ahead and performed the hairdressing ritual. In her own case, she combed back her bangs and then ran away to Hong Kong to work. When she was 24, she returned to Siu Laahm, where her mother said that she must fix her hair either one way or the other, but not just half-way with only the bangs combed back. Her family then held a spinster banquet for her.

———

In some places, constraints on spinsterhood apparently varied by family. One informant, from a multi-surname village between Lohk Chuhng and Sya Gau in Sundak, described the different strategies she and a girl from a neighboring family employed. Her account also further illuminates features of the spinster ritual.

———

In the informant's village, girls usually married at 17 or 18 years of age, but definitely by 20. The informant herself is a spinster. By the time she was 14, she had already told her parents that she didn't want to marry, because marriage arrangements were initiated when girls were about that age. She said that in her village there were both simple and fancy spinster rituals, but most were simple. An auspicious day was selected, and on the morning of the ritual, a girl's hair was combed back into a bun tied with a red string by a "sister" or woman, married or unmarried, of a different surname. It was a rule in her village, the informant said, that the hairdressing ritual could not be performed at home, but only in a house belonging to someone of a different surname.

After the hairdressing ritual, the new spinster donned a skirt for this special occasion—girls and women usually wore pants—and returned home to worship the gods and ancestors. According to the informant, a spinster could worship her father's ancestors only at home, never in the ancestral hall. She said no special gods were worshiped by the spinster, just those usually worshiped in the family. As part of the ritual, the new spinster also had to serve tea to her parents and sisters-in-law. While she served it, her father would say something like, "Now that you've become a spinster, you mustn't do anything to ruin the family's reputation. Don't do anything you aren't supposed to do." The spinster would simply answer, "I know," and that was her vow. According to the informant, that meant that she couldn't change her mind in a few years and marry, creating a scandal—and there were such cases! Then the new spinster gave out red envelopes of good luck money [*leihsih*] to both old and young who were living at home, including muijai. Older female relatives living there might give the spinster a little gift in return, like *leihsih* or a piece of cloth. Afterward, there was a meal, which included roast pork—and always leeks and pig's intestines, because the words for those also meant "everlasting." In a fancier spinster ritual, friends and relatives would gather in the evening for a banquet, bringing gifts like cloth, gold jewelry, face powder, handkerchiefs, and *leihsih*. Sometimes the spinster's "sisters" would come and stay with her the night before the ritual in the house where the hairdressing would be performed. They would stay up late and chat and maybe cook a meal together or fix snacks.

When parents would not allow their daughter to become a spinster, then she had to run away! In the informant's village, the runaway traditionally left behind a sign for her parents so they would know her intentions: red packets, dates, and other fruits were hidden in the rice pot.* The informant remembered the time when a neighbor girl ran away to become a spinster. Her mother, discovering the sign in the rice pot, had come running outside, calling out for her daughter

---

*Another sign that a daughter had decided to become a spinster is described by Topley, who writes that in one village in the Sai Tiuh area of Naahmhoi "the custom was for a woman who learnt of her impending betrothal and wished to remain unattached to dress in her best clothes, and put on a new pair of shoes. She then took two new buckets to the river, and filling them with water brought them home to place before her parents. . . . I could not discover the symbolic significance of this act, but was told that when they saw this they would know her intentions and not dare to stop her" (1973, 13).

and telling everyone her daughter was missing and had run off to become a spinster.

———

Another informant, listening to the above account, interjected that in her village, Pihng Jau in Naahmhoi, spinsterhood was so popular that no one objected when a girl decided to become a spinster.

In contrast to the situation in Pihng Jau, parents in many places did try to prevent their daughters from becoming spinsters. In some places, parents reportedly tried to arrange marriages earlier. In other places, parents would permit only one daughter in the family to become a spinster. Such a situation was described by an informant from Lahk Lauh in Sundak who was the only spinster daughter in her family.

———

The informant was the fourth of five daughters and had one elder and one younger brother. Her three elder sisters had married, the eldest compensating after ten years. The informant wanted to become a spinster but her parents disagreed on whether she should be allowed. Her mother wanted her to marry, but her father, who owned a small silk-reeling workshop, wanted her to become a spinster because she was an especially skillful reeler and helped him in his business. He considered his daughter very "capable." Presumably to discourage marriage suits, her father proceeded to tell others when she was 17 that a match had already been arranged for her. Then when she was 22, he held a spinster banquet for her. On that occasion, the informant recalled, her father was a truly happy man.

The informant explained that there were two economic strategies she could have pursued. Usually, spinsters reeled silk in large factories, where they could make a dollar a day and send money home to their family. In her case, she chose instead to work for her father in his own reeling workshop and live at home. The reelers who worked for her father were paid 40 cents a day; she was paid 20 cents and was proud she could help her father in his business. The informant's younger sister, the fifth daughter, also wanted to become a spinster but was not allowed to. The informant explained that parents in some families would permit only one daughter to become a spinster.

———

Another informant from Lahk Lauh, when asked about a one-spinster-per-family rule, responded that although some people spoke as if there were a such a restriction, it really depended on the family situation. This informant had five paternal aunts who were spinsters and who "taught" her how to be a spinster. She explained that her paternal grandfather liked to have daughters-in-law marry in but didn't like to marry out daughters.

Informants frequently spoke of "learning" to become a spinster from an older female relative, especially a paternal aunt, as in the instance above. Did they also learn to become spinsters from the ballads (*muhk yu syu*) popular in the girls' houses? Asked if those ballads presented unmarried women as role models, most informants responded that there were no unmarried female role models in the ballads they sang. The informants who responded affirmatively, however, remembered only one such ballad, and always the same one: "Gam Jau Eats Vegetarian Food," which tells the story of Gam Jau, who, determined to stay unwed and pure, becomes a Buddhist nun and vegetarian. It thus appears that popular ballads were not a major influence in persuading girls to become spinsters.* Judging from informants' accounts, the primary role models for would-be spinsters were spinster "sisters" and older female relatives, especially paternal aunts.

The second informant from Lahk Lauh above was not the only informant to describe families that boasted several spinster daughters. An informant from a single-surname village near the silk center of Gwai Jau in Sundak told of a paternal uncle with

* It should be noted that a popular deity among women of this area was the Goddess of Mercy, a princess who, as in the story of Gam Jau, resisted marriage to become a Buddhist nun. Topley reports that local religious sects published tracts extolling the virtues of the celibate life (1975, 75–76), but it is unclear whether these circulated among girls of this area (Sankar 1978, 17–18).

two sons and six daughters, four of whom became spinsters. In her village, she explained, spinsters were treated like sons and even received a share in the family estate at the time of its division (*yauh san ga fan*).

Spinsters were often likened to sons with respect to their economic role in natal families. Frequent sojourners in silk and service centers, spinsters supported their families for decades by remitting a portion of their wages home in a pattern reminiscent of sojourning sons. Of course, different economic strategies for spinsters reflected different local economies and constraints on the practice of spinsterhood. Many accounts of successful spinster economic strategies came from the sericultural area. In the silk center of Yuhng Keih in Sundak, for example, an informant reported that nearly every spinster worked as a silk reeler in order to support her family. Informants also provided many accounts of spinsters who supported their families through successful careers as domestic servants. In a typical case, one spinster who supported her family for many years by working as a domestic servant in Hong Kong paid for her parents' funerals and her brothers' weddings and later her nephews' weddings, too. The sociologist Ho It Chong uncovered similar cases in his research among sworn spinsters who immigrated to Singapore (1958, 136).*

Spinsters perceived themselves and were perceived by others as quintessentially "capable" women (*hou bunsih*). By popular definition, spinsters had to be capable women, able at the very least to support themselves. However, capability was measured in more than wage contributions. Despite the stereotype of spinsters as wage earners engaged in lucrative employment in the silk and service industries, many spinsters engaged in other, less profitable activities. These spinsters often contributed to their natal family through a combination of income from wages and direct labor input in family enterprises. For example, in

---

*For further discussion of sworn spinsters as silk reelers and domestic servants, see Chapter 8. For more information on sworn spinsters in domestic service in Singapore and Hong Kong, see Ho 1958; Topley 1958; and Sankar 1978.

A farmhouse with attached shed for rearing silkworms. Note the mulberry trees around the house, the easy access to water transport, and the isolated setting of the house. (Howard and Buswell 1925, plate IV)

A maid from the Canton Delta (John Thomson, *Illustrations of China*, 1873)

Two married women (above and top right) from the Canton Delta (John
Thomson, *Illustrations of China*, 1873)

Women reeling cocoons inside a steam filature in Kwangtung (lower
right). Behind them are reels of silk thread and overhead a bag of cocoons. (Howard and Buswell 1925, plate III)

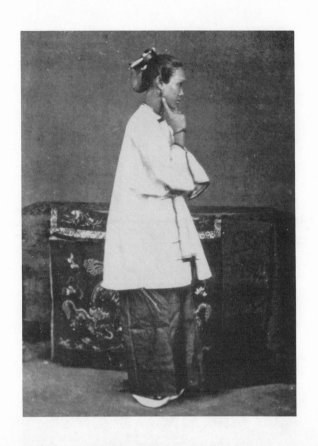

A bride and groom from the Canton Delta (John Thomson, *Illustrations of China*, 1873)

A married woman attended by her maid. The child may be her daughter. Note the differences in hair styles. (John Thomson, *Illustrations of China*, 1873)

Jung Chyun in Punyu, although most spinsters reportedly left to work as domestic servants in Hong Kong, some stayed in the village, where they worked in various capacities, including harvesting and carrying peanuts, preparing and drying olives, and cutting and drying sweet potatoes. In Bik Gong in Sundak, those spinsters who did not leave the village for Hong Kong engaged in the production of ritual money.

In a finely drawn life history provided by Andrea Sankar, a 79-year-old sworn spinster from Luhng Saan in Sundak describes the several economic strategies that she employed to earn money to pay for her spinster ceremony. This account also further highlights the role of paternal aunts and "sisters" in shaping a girl's decision to become a sworn spinster.

When I was 16, I did not yet understand that I must resist marriage. My parents tried to arrange a marriage for me then. They did not tell me about it because they were afraid I might run off like other girls I knew. Actually, I was too ignorant to do so at that time. Fortunately, the wedding was called off because we had a dispute over the size of the ceremony. The groom's family, which had to pay for the banquet, sought to limit the number of dinner tables and guests, while my family wanted to invite more people. Then my paternal aunt, who was a spinster, and my elder sisters in the girls' house told me I must resist marriage. If a girl is forced to marry before she is old enough to understand these things, then her sisters will not abandon her but will instead help and comfort her if her marriage is difficult. But if a girl willingly marries, then her sisters will despise her and she can never again turn to them for help. . . .

When I was 19, I had a dream that my mother was again trying to arrange a marriage for me. Fortunately I understood what I had to do and was prepared. I went before my parents and told them I knew of their plans. They were shocked because a young girl is not supposed to know these things, and they did not understand how I found out. I told my parents that I refused to marry and that if they proceeded, they would have to repay the price of the wedding because I would never go to a husband. Then I said that to make me marry was like cutting off their arm, because I was such a valuable worker. They were silent for a long time, then my mother said, "Very well, but you must promise to behave yourself." I planned to hold my hair-combing ceremony as soon as I could save enough money, but my father died four months later and we all went into mourning for three years.

During those three years, I was able to save a lot of money. I would save 100 *yüan* and put them in a coin roll. I bought gold jewelry, bracelets, and earrings. I also loaned my money to the neighbors for 20 *fen* interest a month. In our area, we had to pay all the rent in cash at the end of each year. Often the neighbors were short, so I helped them until the silk harvests came in. Sometimes people just needed money to buy furniture or rebuild their house. The silk industry was growing more and more prosperous, and wages continued to rise. When I first started working for neighbors in 1914, I earned 20 to 30 *fen* a day for *cho gaan* [a role in silk making], which increased by 1922 to 50 or 60 *fen* a day. I could then earn 90 *fen* to a *yüan* a day for spinning, 80 *fen* for picking mulberry leaves, or 40 *fen* for gathering firewood and cutting grass. Labor was so much in demand that the factories had to give bonuses to keep people working. These bonuses were called *kahn gung*. For every 14 consecutive days you worked, you got two and a half days' extra pay. It probably sounds like a lot of people would have wanted to work in the factories because of this extra money. But this wasn't so. The work was very hard; you only got a half-hour break for lunch. Besides, a good spinner could earn as much or more working for her neighbors.

After three years, the mourning period was over, and I had enough money to pay for my celibacy ceremony. My aunt (my father's sister) who was also a spinster told me that the hair-combing ceremony should be a very important occasion. "If you have money," she said, "you should spend most of it on the ceremony because it is very important and only happens once in a girl's life."

The sou hei [*sohei*] ceremony is similar to a marriage ceremony. Your friends and your relatives come. All the guests bring gifts. Mine was very grand; many people came. Many older spinster women came. People gave me gold rings and bracelets and household things like bedding and wash basins. The banquet was held at my mother's home. There were nine dinner tables and nearly 100 guests. Two of the tables were occupied with guards and guns, because my relatives and the people in the village were rich. They worked hard and had their savings in gold, so the village needed many guards.

I paid for the whole celebration except for the rice, which my mother gave. The banquet cost me 100 *yüan*. I bought a lot of long buns to distribute to the guests informing them of the celebrations. Women who are about to marry also distribute cakes to relatives and friends. After giving out the long buns, I went to the temple of Kuan Yin, the Goddess of Mercy, to worship. Every spinster must worship Kuan Yin because she is a woman and remained unwed. I went to the temple alone to worship for the hair-combing ceremony and brought a lot of food as offering to the goddess; mainly I gave her chicken backs. I also offered chicken backs and tea to my ancestors in the ancestor hall. After I returned home, I paid my respects to my mother and offered her a cup of tea. I would have done this for both of my parents if my father had been alive. Then my *kai ma* [godmother] dressed my hair as a married woman's.

On the second night there was a banquet. My sisters stayed at home to play mah-jongg. Some sisters and cousins came from other villages; a few of these were sisters who had married. In the village where my cousins lived, they did not have to work. They were able to read; they had leisure time and could be educated. My cousins were rich because their father was in business. Their village was far away, and they had to come by boat and sedan chair. Some of my friends who had been married off to other villages returned for the ceremony. (Sankar 1984, 56–58)

RESIDENCE IN LIFE AND DEATH

In some cases, as we have seen, spinsters who contributed labor to family economic enterprises lived at home. The spinsters cited earlier who stayed in Jung Chyun and Bik Gong reportedly lived natolocally. However, meeting family economic obligations—even through direct labor contributions to family economic enterprises—did not guarantee that spinster daughters could claim natolocal residence.

Many places imposed constraints on natolocal residence for spinsters. In some cases, constraints were based on an assumed disharmony between spinsters and the co-resident wives of brothers and uncles. In the single-surname village of Bak Muhn San Gei outside Daaih Leuhng in Sundak, there was a general proscription against natolocal residence for all village spinsters. An informant explained that people thought it inappropriate for spinsters to live at home when wives of brothers were in residence. In other places, such as Chahn Chyun in Sundak, a similar residence constraint depended on individual family dynamics. An informant explained that if the wives of her uncles did not object, a spinster was allowed to live at home; if they did, she had to make other arrangements.

Spinsters in some places were treated like married daughters with regard to natolocal residence. Thus, even where they were permitted to live at home, spinsters were sometimes subject to the same restrictions that applied to married daughters. For example, in a single-surname village in Daaih Sya in Naahmhoi county, spinsters were usually permitted to live at home, even during most festival times. However, at the Lunar New Year, they were required to leave home, as were married daughters, and were forbidden to pass the festival period on village land. Another informant, reacting to this account, reported that in her single-surname village in Gong Meih in Sundak spinsters lived at home even during the New Year.

A still more critical constraint on the natolocal residence of spinsters was the common prohibition against spinsters' dying at home. With respect to place of residence at death, spinsters were generally treated more like unmarried daughters than like married daughters or sons. Even where spinsters were permitted to reside natolocally during their productive years, they were often required to make other provisions for old age, periods of illness, and death. The death of a daughter who was unmarried and thus without an affiliation to a male descent line was troubling to her natal family. A "hostless" daughter was not allowed to die in the main house, but was either removed to an outlying building, a shed, or empty house, or, in the sericultural area, taken out onto the levees. Other appropriate places for dying hostless women were special structures or temples, in essence death houses, situated on the outskirts of a village. These were variously called *che gung miuh, fongbihn so,* or *sinleuhng miuh.*

A family's unease over the death of an unmarried daughter continued after her death, for her hostless spirit was considered potentially disruptive of the family and its fortunes. Informants explained that the remedy for a deceased daughter's hostless condition was, of course, to secure her a host. This was achieved through one variety of spirit marriage, *gwai ga gwai,* in which the spirit of a deceased unmarried woman was married to a deceased unmarried man (see Chapter 5). However, even in death, the proper sibling order was observed in the marriage of children. Thus, a marriage was not immediately arranged for a deceased daughter if she was not of marriageable age and if she had older unmarried siblings. Instead, the deceased unmarried daughter was given a temporary paper tablet, placed not on the domestic altar but in a corner near the door (*deih jyuh geuk*). The daughter's spirit then awaited its turn to marry; at the proper time, a matchmaker was engaged to arrange a marriage with a suitable deceased man.

Spinsters who were treated like unmarried daughters *at* death and not allowed to die at home were also treated like unmarried daughters *after* death. That is, along with the prohibition against spinsters dying in natal homes was a prohibition against the placement of spinster tablets on domestic altars in those natal homes. Thus, where the metaphor of spinsters as unmarried daughters held for spinsters at death, it held after death as well.

The twin prohibition against death and tablet placement in natal homes was the most commonly occurring pattern. However, informants from a few villages scattered across the delayed transfer marriage area were treated like sons at death. Spinsters in Pihng Jau and Hah Paak in Naahmhoi, Mah Gong and Gong Meih Ching Chah in Sundak, Siu Bak in Punyu, and Siu Laahm and Waih Hau in Jungsaan were allowed to die at home. Informants from these villages were aware that in other places, citing Yuhng Keih, Gwai Jau, and Daaih Leuhng in Sundak, spinsters were not allowed to die at home. In cases where the metaphor of spinsters as sons held at death, it did not necessarily hold after death. That is, the tablets of spinsters permitted to die at home were allowed to be kept at home only in some places. In other places, the spinster had to make alternative arrangements for the placement of her tablet.

In at least one village the spinster-as-son metaphor was complete, with spinsters being treated consistently as sons in residence during life, residence at death, and placement of tablet after death:

———

On the outskirts of Siu Laahm in Jungsaan, in an area devoted to the cultivation of rice and mulberry, was the multi-surname village of Waih Hau. Girls in Waih Hau earned wages harvesting mulberry leaves and raising silkworms for other families when their own family harvests were done. Mulberry leaves and cocoons were primarily exported, and silk reeling was limited to simple hand reeling of "extra" cocoons at home. The informant had three sisters who became spinsters. She explained that girls married before the age of 20 or, if they became spinsters, took their spinster vows after 20. Parents would not allow girls under 20 to become spinsters, but they did not force daughters to marry. A girl could decide for herself whether marriage or spinsterhood best suited her. Few spinsters left Waih Hau, most staying in the village and living at home. These spinsters contributed to their family, but still managed to save some of their earnings for themselves. According to the informant, spinsters in Waih Hau were "like sons." Not only did they live at home, spinsters were also permitted to die at home—and their tablets were placed in the ancestral hall together with the male ancestors [*go sahnjyupaaih ngon hai chitohng tuhngmaaih di jousin yatchai*].

In some places spinsters, again like sons, inherited a share of the family estate on the death of their parents (*yauh san ga fan*).

The informant was from Gwai Jau Ngoih Chyun in Sundak. When asked whether a spinster could live at home if a sister-in-law was already in residence, she replied, "Yes, because a spinster was the same as a son and inherited a share in the family estate." She said that a spinster in Ngoih Chyun could even inherit agricultural fields and land. She added that, of course, only well-to-do families left property to their children. In poor families there was no land to inherit, even for sons.

On death, spinsters themselves usually left their property to their natal family, but in some cases they left it to adopted daughters. Spinsters were sometimes given girls to raise as adopted daughters who would care for them in old age and tend their tablets after death. Sometimes girls who were bought as muijai, to be raised and sold as secondary wives, were kept by their spinster-employers as adopted daughters. Adopted daughters of spinsters were themselves raised to become spinsters. Some informants even spoke of a preference among spinsters for taking an agnatic niece, that is, a brother's daughter, as their adopted daughter. The preference for an agnatic niece as adopted daughter, heir, and successor is significant since it undoubtedly served to reinforce a spinster's affiliation with her father's descent line.

A few informants provided data on mourning dress that can be used to further differentiate spinster daughters from unmarried daughters, married daughters, and daughters-in-law. Although mourning dress for the different categories of daughter varied somewhat by place, informants consistently responded that the mourning ritual required of spinster daughters for deceased parents was like that expected of sons with respect to the required length of time in mourning. For sons as well as for spinsters, a full three-year period of color avoidance in dress was required. An informant from a single-surname village in Punyu, Sya Hoh Cheuhng Beng, reported that only daughters who were spinsters wore mourning for three years. The informant, a spinster, said that her mother told the family on her deathbed that her spinster daughter should mourn her as a son.

SPINSTER HOUSES

Clearly the disposition of the spinster at death and of her spirit and tablet after death was a major constraint on natolocal residence for spinsters and hence on the practice of spinsterhood. Remedies for the hostless plight of spinsters varied in kind and availability over time and space, but the spinster house (*gupoh nguk*) was the generally preferred solution. Spinster houses, frequently owned by the spinsters themselves, provided a home for the ill or dying spinster and a place for her tablet after death. In places where there were constraints on natolocal residence, the spinster house was often the designated residence for spinsters. For many spinsters, however, residence in a spinster house was preferable to residence with their natal family. Spinster houses were reminiscent of girls' houses. In some places the two institutions were quite distinct. In other places, primarily towns and prosperous villages—for example, the towns of Daaih Leuhng, Yuhng Keih, Gwai Jau, and Chahn Chyun in Sundak—the two kinds of houses merged in identity and overlapped in function. An informant from Daaih Leuhng observed that girls' houses as separate institutions were usually found only in small villages.

In villages where spinster houses and girls' houses were distinct, the distinctions were impressive. As we have seen, girls' houses were a traditional feature of Delta villages and were typically extra houses owned by families and situated on family land. Spinster houses, by contrast, were usually built or bought by the spinsters themselves. In some places, spinster houses could not be situated on family land or within village boundaries. An informant from Lahm Ngohk in Naahmhoi explained that spinsters were like married daughters, and therefore, people felt they should not continue to live on family land. According to the informant, even when buying land on which to build a spinster house, spinsters had to be careful not to "frighten" people and bring them bad luck.

The practice of sworn spinsterhood was to some extent constrained by the availability of spinster houses. Spinster houses were not found in every village or in every generation. Informants often spoke of spinsters and spinster houses interchangeably, answering questions about spinsters in terms of spinster houses, and vice-versa. For example, when queried whether there were many spinsters in her village, one informant answered, "No, because there were no spinster houses." Another, when asked about spinster houses, replied, "There were only a few in my village but many in a nearby village where there were many spinsters." Some informants elaborated on the relationship between spinsters and spinster houses:

One informant was from a small village in the Sai Tiuh area of Naahmhoi, where most families farmed; only one or two families engaged in sericulture, producing mulberry leaves and cocoons for export to silk-reeling centers. According to the informant, spinsters could not die at home but were required to go to a spinster house. However, there was no spinster house in the village, and the informant explained that this was one reason why there were so few spinsters. She said another reason was that it was difficult for spinsters to make a living from farming.

Spinster houses were further distinguished from girls' houses on the basis of recruitment. Residence in a spinster house required financial means and therefore depended on a spinster's economic success. A spinster had to have the means to buy, build, or rent a spinster house—or to buy a share or rent a room in an established spinster house. One Sundak spinster, whose description of her elaborate spinster ceremony is cited above, related the experience and expense incurred by one group of "sisters" in building a spinster house.

A father cannot allow his spinster daughter to live in her natal home, because after the celibacy ceremony she is considered "married" and married women are forbidden to die at home. If she dies within her own kin group, then all the bad things that happen to her family will be blamed on her spirit. Instead, she can live only in a spinster house, and that house is the only place for her to die. A spinster must also build her spinster house in a different surname section from that of her family. In my village there were several surname sections.

I built my spinster house together with several sisters. One was my godmother, one was her younger sister, and the other was my *kai neuih* [goddaughter]. It took us a long time to get the spinster house built; it cost us 180 *yüan*. We bought bricks from a rich man who kept having to sell the bricks from his house to pay his gambling debts. We also got some building materials from another man who needed money and sold us an old building, which we had to pull down ourselves. After we collected enough materials to build a house, we hired a group of builders and paid for a shed so they could rest and eat in the shade. Of course, they paid us rent for the shed. But they were too slow and could not finish the house. We hired another man, but he just ran off with our money. Finally we hired a third group. This time *we* paid the rent for the shed; it cost us 10 *yüan* a month. We ran out of money, and I had to borrow many *yüan* from my mother so we could finish. When we moved in, we had a joyful *yahp fo* [entering] ceremony. All our friends came to help us move our possessions in. (Sankar 1984, 58–59)

Spinsters working in villages where there were constraints on living natolocally could live in spinster houses full-time. Even where they were permitted to live natolocally, many spinsters who could afford it preferred to live in a spinster house, where they enjoyed greater freedom. Ho reports that in some places there was peer pressure to live independently of parents and that spinsters who lived at home were laughed at and called "boneless" (1958, 58).

For those spinsters who migrated to larger villages and towns for employment, one common strategy was to build a spinster house back in their natal village or buy a share in one already established there. A spinster-sojourner could visit her spinster house whenever she liked and eventually return to live there on retirement.

Where spinsters could neither die nor have their tablets placed at home, the spinster without funds for a spinster house found herself in desperate straits. Without a spinster house, she was hostless and, on death, was taken either to one of the wayside structures for unmarried women or to a mountain top or other remote place. An informant reported that in Yuhng Keih in Sundak a spinster could not die at home, but that if she had money, she could go to a spinster house and have her tablet placed there after death. Without funds for a spinster house, however, she was taken to a grass hut to die. Another informant, from Gong Meih in Sundak, reported that if a spinster did not have funds for a spinster house, her tablet was taken outside the village and placed in a wayside temple [*che gung miuh*].

For most spinsters without a spinster house to retire to, the future was indeed bleak. The prospect of dying in a wayside temple or in some remote and inhospitable place was frightening. A tablet placed at a remove from the community of spinsters in the spinster house was easily neglected and left untended. There was, however, another remedy to the hostless plight of the spinster, one that was both a more affordable and a more traditional means of securing a host than the spinster house. This remedy was a special variant of spirit marriage, often called buying an entrance or host (*maaih muhn hau*), which I consider in the following chapter.

5

Arranging
a Spirit Marriage

Spirit marriage—a posthumous marriage in which one part-
ner or both are deceased—was practiced within both the major-
marriage and the delayed transfer marriage systems. Although
various kinds of spirit marriage have been reported for traditional Chinese society, no analysis of the regional variation in
the practice has yet been undertaken.* Within the delayed transfer marriage area, I found several different varieties of spirit
marriage, each reflecting a different configuration of circumstances, parties, and interests. One of these varieties—what I
call "bride-initiated spirit marriage"—has not been reported elsewhere and appears unique to the delayed transfer marriage area.
Bride-initiated spirit marriage constitutes still another marriage-
resistance practice.

I begin by considering the full spectrum of spirit marriages
reported by informants for the delayed transfer marriage area,

*For additional information on spirit marriage in traditional Chinese society,
see Freedman 1970; Ahern 1973; and A. Wolf 1974.

in order to provide the context for a fuller discussion of bride-initiated spirit marriage. On the basis of when marriage was arranged, spirit marriages described for this area can be divided into two main categories. On the further basis of the status of each of the parties to the marriage, two varieties of spirit marriage can be identified within each of these categories.

VARIETIES

The first category consisted of spirit marriages arranged before the death of either party, the marriage of a living bride to a spirit groom who is her deceased fiancé or the marriage of a living groom to his deceased fiancée. The death of either bride or groom before marriage did not automatically abrogate a marriage agreement, and the spirit of the deceased was frequently married to the surviving party. The surviving bride who proceeded with the marriage was usually required to observe some degree of mourning for her deceased groom, which entailed participation in the funeral ritual and adherence to strict standards of dress and conduct in the following years. Informants reported that because of the many restrictions involved in this kind of spirit marriage, including immediate virilocal residence, brides usually did not want to marry their deceased fiancés. Called *sau ching*, the marriage of a bride to her deceased fiancé was in effect the accommodation of marriage to the changed circumstances occasioned by death. This variety of spirit marriage did not constitute an alternative marriage strategy or a marriage-resistance practice.

The second main category of spirit marriage in the delayed transfer area consisted of spirit marriages arranged posthumously. In one variant in this category—"ghost marries ghost" (*gwai ga gwai*)—a spirit bride was married to a spirit groom. Such a marriage was a traditional remedy for several conditions, including the hostless condition of a deceased unmarried woman, the heirless condition of a deceased unmarried man, and the general restlessness of the spirits of the unmarried dead.

For parents of a deceased daughter, a "ghost marries ghost" spirit marriage secured for their daughter an affiliation to a male descent line, which provided her with a host for her spirit and tablet, and averted problems like crop failure or infertility that her otherwise unattached spirit might cause the living. Parents of a deceased son sought through such a spirit marriage to facilitate the adoption of an heir and successor for their son. As in the marriage of a surviving bride or groom to a deceased fiancé, a "ghost marries ghost" spirit marriage did not constitute a marriage strategy, but was in effect the extension of marriage beyond death.

The second variety of spirit marriage within this category was bride-initiated spirit marriage, which was a marriage-resistance practice. In this variety of spirit marriage, a living bride married the spirit of a deceased groom who had *predeceased* the arrangement of marriage.* Like compensation marriage and sworn spinsterhood, this kind of spirit marriage constituted an alternative strategy for women disinclined to marry in the customary fashion. As popularly practiced in the delayed transfer marriage area by both spinsters and unmarried girls, this variety of spirit marriage was frequently initiated by the brides themselves, for whom it was a strategy of special advantage. For spinsters, bride-initiated spirit marriage was a means of acquiring a host for their spirit and tablet. For unmarried girls who for various reasons were not allowed to become spinsters, bride-initiated spirit marriage was an alternative to delayed transfer marriage that had even more advantages than compensation marriage.

Bride-initiated spirit marriage was frequently described as being desired and arranged by the women themselves (*jihgei yuhnyi ge* and *jihgei wan ge*). It did not occur throughout the delayed transfer marriage area, but was found primarily in places where the other marriage-resistance practices occurred, especially in Sundak county. What I am calling "bride-initiated spirit marriage" was, in fact, known to informants by several names. It was usually called "fake" spirit marriage (*mouh ching*)—per-

---

*No spirit marriages in which a living groom married a spirit bride who *predeceased* the arrangement of marriage were reported.

haps because the bride did not participate in mourning for her husband—sometimes it was known simply as *baahk ching*. Informants also referred to this kind of spirit marriage as "marrying a spirit tablet" (*ga sahnjyupaaih*) since the bride married the spirit of a deceased man as embodied in his spirit tablet. Sundak informants often spoke of bride-initiated spirit marriage as "buying an entrance" (*maaih muhn hau*), in essence "buying a host."* For both spinsters and unmarried girls, bride-initiated spirit marriage provided a host for spirit and tablet, but the motivations for arranging these marriages differed.

HOSTS AND HEIRS

As described in the last chapter, spinster houses were a remedy for the hostless condition of spinsters. A spinster without the financial resources for a spinster house was left with no provision for her spirit and tablet. However, financial resources were not the only factors affecting access to spinster houses, which varied over space and time. In some places in the delayed transfer marriage area, there were no spinster houses. In other places, the number of spinster houses increased over time. Informants aged 65 to 80 in 1980 reported that from mother's generation to informant's own generation, the number of spinster houses increased and the frequency of spinster-initiated spirit marriages decreased. Only one informant, a 90-year-old woman from Yuhng Keih in Sundak, reported that it was popular for spinsters to marry tablets in her own generation. Another 90-year-old informant, from Seui Tuhng in Sundak, said that spinsters in her generation married tablets in order to acquire ancestors (*seung wan go jou*). Among informants under 80, bride-initiated spirit marriage was perceived as more common among women of an older generation. A 69-year-old informant from Bik Gong in Sundak reported that more spinsters married spirits in

*Alfred Fabre also uses the expression *maaih muhn hau* in an article on customs in Sundak (1935, 114). He reports that a celibate aunt (apparently a paternal aunt) sometimes married a tablet in order to secure a place to die and an altar for her tablet.

the preceding generation, "when families wanted their spinster daughters to have a proper place to die and an altar for their tablet after death." A 77-year-old Sundak informant from Gwai Jau Ngoih Chyun explained that no spinster in her own generation married a spirit because "spinsterhood was *like marriage* and there was no need to marry after becoming a spinster."

These accounts suggest that few spirit marriages were contracted by spinsters in the informants' own generation, that is, after around 1920. Spinsters who did contract spirit marriages had no access to a spinster house, either because they could not afford it or because there were none. In other cases, spinsters or their parents did not feel that spinster houses provided as proper a host as marriage, even marriage to a tablet.

Unmarried girls who contracted spirit marriages were said to be girls whose parents would not allow them to become spinsters. Bride-initiated spirit marriage represented for these girls a second-best alternative to delayed transfer marriage. Informants described it as a "way to avoid marriage." Some parents preferred spirit marriage over sworn spinsterhood for their daughters for the same reasons some spinsters endorsed it: it was a way to secure a host through more traditional means. In a case cited in the last chapter, an informant from Lahk Lauh in Sundak recounted how her father had allowed her but not her younger sister to become a spinster. She also explained her sister's fate.

Although the informant's sister had been strongly opposed to marriage, her family had not allowed her to become a spinster. Therefore, she contracted a spirit marriage as an alternative to customary marriage. The informant explained that since two spinsters were not allowed in one house, if one daughter had already become a spinster, then the next had to "marry a tablet" in order to stay unmarried.

Although many unmarried girls reportedly turned to spirit marriage when unable to become spinsters, demography did constrain the practice of this form of marriage. As one informant summed up the situation, "It was not so easy to find an unmarried dead man to marry!" When a family of a deceased son decided to arrange his marriage, the news spread quickly. A Sundak informant recalled discussing with several other village girls the availability of a certain deceased man for marriage. One of the girls was very eager to contract a spirit marriage and started shouting, "I'll go, I'll go!" A Punyu informant similarly reported that when girls heard that a deceased man was available for marriage, "they struggled among themselves to be the one who would get to marry him!"

For some parents, spirit marriages were an attractive remedy to the hostless plight of spinster daughters and an acceptable marriage alternative for unmarried daughters who, though disinclined to marry, were unable to become spinsters. For parents of deceased sons, spirit marriage was a means to acquire an heir for their son. A family contracted a spirit marriage for their deceased son in order to provide him with a wife and adopt a grandchild—an heir for their son—from among patrilineally related male children. Informants called spirit marriage a "way to continue the family." Thus, in general, whereas a hostless condition motivated spinsters and unmarried girls and their families to contract spirit marriages, an heirless condition motivated the families of deceased sons.

A concern with acquiring heirs was inextricably bound up with a concern over the disposition of property. It was predominantly propertied families, informants reported, who were concerned with arranging this kind of spirit marriage for a deceased son. Providing a deceased son with a wife was a precursor to adopting an heir for him who would inherit property. Families with no property could not support daughters-in-law and heirs. Poor families could not attract an heir or arrange to adopt a male child of patrilineally related kin. Such families were therefore unable to arrange this kind of spirit marriage. Families too poor to secure an heir for a deceased son or concerned only with preserving proper sibling order in the marriage of children—even a deceased child had to be married before his younger siblings could be—pursued a different strategy. They contracted a "ghost marries ghost" spirit marriage (*gwai ga gwai*) in which the spirit of their son was married to the spirit of a deceased woman. An informant from Daaih Leuhng in Sundak offered further insight into the motivations behind the arrangement of bride-initiated spirit marriages.

―――――

The informant explained that *mouh ching* was for girls who didn't want to marry and needed to find a host [*yiu wan muhn hau*]. She said the groom's family was usually well-to-do and the mother wanted to arrange a marriage for her deceased son in order to adopt an heir for him [*sihng gai jai*]. The informant explained that sometimes a mother was afraid that persons in her husband's family would deceive her and occupy her property. She therefore contracted a spirit marriage for her deceased son and adopted a son for him, a kind of adopted grandson for her.

―――――

These illuminating comments suggest that spirit marriage was sometimes a strategy on the part of married women and widows to protect their property from appropriation by other family and lineage members and thus make their own old age secure. They also suggest the relative advantages of two different strategies for protecting property and acquiring heirs in a family without sons. A family with no sons would in most cases simply adopt a male child of patrilineal kin. In a family with no surviving sons but with a deceased one, two strategies were possible. Again, the family could simply adopt a male child as their own son. Or, they could marry in a wife for their deceased son and adopt a son for him (a grandson for them). In both strategies, the preferred child for adoption was a male child of patrilineal kin, called a *sihng gai jai*. In contrast to simple adoption, however, spirit marriage introduced members of two generations to the family, both a daughter-in-law and a grandson. In a society characterized by powerful lineages, this kind of spirit marriage may have provided individual families or widows of deceased sons added security for their property.

Most informants did not express a bias against bride-initiated spirit marriage, but a few did. One Punyu informant was from Fo Chyun, a village from within the delayed transfer area where compensation marriage and sworn spinsterhood were not practiced. Bride-initiated spirit marriage also was not practiced in Fo Chyun, and the informant called it a "stupid" practice that occurred only in Sundak, "where women had a lot of money."

One informant was from a single-surname village in Naahmhoi Sai Tiuh in the delayed transfer area. The village economy depended on the cultivation of rice and turnips, although one or two families raised mulberry trees. Girls helped families farm and sometimes went to nearby villages to plant rice seedlings. The informant, a married woman, said she had never heard of compensation marriage in the village. In addition, she said there were very few sworn spinsters in her own generation, and only one or two in her mother's generation. The village had a girls' house but no spinster house, and spinsters had to go to another village to die. She described four types of spirit marriage, *dihng ching, sau ching, laahk saan,* and *mouh ching.** Of these, she said that *mouh ching,* or "fake spirit marriage," was the lowest form. In this form, a mother-in-law did not even have to have sons but only a lot of heritable property [*yauh san ga fan*]. The

---

*According to the informant, *dihng ching* was a spirit marriage arranged when a baby son died soon after birth. This kind of spirit marriage ensured that the deceased son's line continued (*dihng muhn hau, dihng sahnjyupaaih*). However, its main purpose, according to the informant, was to marry in a daughter-in-law to care for the mother. A banquet celebrated a *dihng ching* spirit marriage; however, the bride did not ride to her husband's home in a red sedan chair (*daaih huhng fa giu*) but in a green one (*ching yi giu*) instead. *Sau ching* was a marriage between a living bride and her deceased fiancé. The bride in a *sau ching* marriage was already engaged to the deceased at the time of his death and had eaten the engagement cakes at *gwo mahn dihng*. According to the informant, this kind of spirit marriage was the noblest kind because a bride in *sau ching* participated in the formal mourning ritual for the deceased groom. In another form of spirit marriage called *laahk saan,* a living bride married the spirit of her deceased fiancé several days or weeks after his burial, but did not participate in the mourning ritual. According to the informant, a *laahk saan* spirit marriage was inferior to *sau ching.* There was no wedding banquet, and the bride was conveyed to the groom's home in a green sedan chair.

mother-in-law, at her own convenience, arranged for the spirit marriage to take place. And the only reason a bride agreed to marry in this fashion was because she wanted a *muhn hau* ["host"] and a place to die.

RITUALS AND RESIDENCE

One of the most variable features of bride-initiated spirit marriage was the exchange of bridewealth and dowry; informants variously reported that in this form of spirit marriage, families exchanged small amounts of bridewealth and dowry, dowry but no bridewealth, bridewealth but no dowry, and neither bride-wealth nor dowry but just red money packets (*leihsih*). Several informants reported that the groom's family gave the bride a house (*yauh gaan nguk bei go sanneung*). Bridewealth and dowry were apparently very negotiable in bride-initiated spirit mar-riages, more so than in delayed transfer marriages. No custom-ary figures were quoted as in the case of marriage, but evidence suggests that this kind of spirit marriage was affordable for brides and their families. In fact, in some cases the bridewealth was substantially greater than the dowry, and some families and their spinster daughters who contracted spirit marriages were said to be "greedy" for bridewealth.

Marriage ritual was much simplified in bride-initiated spirit marriage. There was reportedly no bridal sedan chair or elabo-rate display and feasting as in the case of delayed transfer mar-riage. The core features of the marriage ritual were the worship by the bride of her husband's ancestors and the gods and the serving of tea to her parents-in-law. In contrast to *sau ching*, the variety of spirit marriage in which a bride married the spirit of her deceased fiancé, no mourning for the deceased spouse was required of brides in bride-initiated spirit marriages.

Highly variable bridewealth and dowry arrangements in these spirit marriages initially seemed matched by equally vari-able postmarital residence arrangements for brides. The most common response to questions about residence in bride-initiated spirit marriages was "it depends." As the research progressed, however, the meaning behind this qualified response became clear: in residence pattern, bride-initiated spirit marriage was modeled on delayed transfer marriage. Bridedaughters in these spirit marriages sometimes lived natolocally, sometimes virilocally, and sometimes egolocally or independently (while employed away from home), depending on the point in the postmarital residence cycle. As in delayed transfer marriages, residence for bridedaughters in these spirit marriages was initially natolocal and only later virilocal. In bride-initiated spirit marriages, too, bridedaughters were required to visit their husband's home from time to time during the period of natolocal residence. These visits were scheduled on festival or family occasions, including the anniversary of the husband's death.

Residence in bride-initiated spirit marriage was, however, more flexible than in the case of delayed transfer marriage; some informants said that the bridedaughter could do as she pleased, settling with her husband's family at any time that suited her. Some bridedaughters went to live in their husband's home only in old age or at death, as in the case of compensation marriage. Others reportedly went much earlier, especially if they were comfortable with their husband's family.

An informant from Bik Gong in Sundak explained that a bride in *mouh ching* did not have to live with her husband's family at first, but she had to visit on birthdays, death days, and weddings. She could settle with them at any time she liked. If she got along with her husband's uncles and brothers, then she usually went to live with them earlier. The informant reported that in this kind of spirit marriage there was always an adopted son [*sihng gai jai*], who lived with the husband's family even when his "mother" did not.

As in the case of compensation marriage, the continuity of the male descent line—the reproductive goal of the husband's family—was not dependent on claims to the wife's fertility. The wife in a bride-initiated spirit marriage was expected to live a chaste life. Although she herself did not produce an heir for her husband's family, she was a social instrument for acquiring one. With her marriage to their deceased son, her husband's family claimed a "grandson" by adoption.

Evidently the bridedaughter's release from a reproductive obligation in spirit marriage allowed her some flexibility in residence. Informants' accounts are free of any mention of peer pressure on bridedaughters in spirit marriages to prolong intervals of natolocal residence. There was no tension over sexual behavior or fertility as in delayed transfer marriages, and therefore no reported ridicule by "sisters" to deter early assumption of virilocal residence.

For bridedaughters in spirit marriages, the pattern of production was also reminiscent of delayed transfer marriage. Bridedaughters worked and saved their own wages to support themselves. In fact, unmarried girls were motivated to contract spirit marriages in order to gain license to earn their own living (*jih sihk keih lihk*). While living and working independently of her husband's family, a bridedaughter was not dependent on them for support. The most commonly mentioned sources of employment for bridedaughters in spirit marriages were silk reeling and domestic service. For example, an informant from Chahn Chyun in Sundak reported many spirit marriages among silk workers in her village. Another informant, from Daaih Leuhng in Sundak, when asked where a bride resided in a spirit marriage, responded "it depends" and went on to say that a bride might live with her parents or her mother-in-law or "work as a domestic servant."

All the forms of marriage resistance discussed here—compensation marriage, sworn spinsterhood, and spirit marriage—were influenced and shaped by the customary form of marriage in the Canton Delta, delayed transfer. In compensation marriage, a woman negotiated to retain her status as a bridedaughter and her rights as primary wife while avoiding or postponing cohabitation with her husband and his family. In essence, she delayed the transfer beyond the objectionable stage of marriage. A sworn spinster opted out of marriage altogether, but her subsequent life was affected by her natal family's and her natal village's interpretation of her status in relation to that of a bride-daughter/wife in a delayed transfer marriage. A woman who initiated a spirit marriage in effect contracted a delayed transfer marriage with a dead man. The important point here is that all three practices were forms of marriage resistance, but delayed transfer marriage was not, even though outsiders frequently misperceived it as a form of marriage resistance.

6

Delayed Transfer Marriage, Cultural Prejudice, and Political Repression

As we have seen, delayed transfer marriage was the customary and dominant form of marriage in an extensive area of the Canton Delta. The core area of the delayed transfer marriage extended southward from Canton, unbroken by villages practicing major marriage except in the immediate vicinity of Canton. Canton itself presented a mix of marriage systems. Why did Canton and its immediate environs break the pattern of delayed transfer marriage?

The practice of delayed transfer marriage was affected by the salient political reality that the delayed transfer marriage area was part of the Chinese empire, in which the Confucian ideal, or major marriage, was the *orthodox* marriage form. Delayed transfer marriage marked local culture, but major marriage marked national culture. Consequently delayed transfer marriage was subject to cultural prejudice and political repression that shaped not only its practice but also the perception of that marriage system and its portrayal in the literature.

Informants reported that women from within the delayed transfer marriage system who married into the major-marriage system were absorbed into the more orthodox system. One Sundak informant described her marriage to a man from Seiwui county:

The informant was from Yuhng Keih in Sundak in the delayed transfer marriage area, but she had married a man from outside that area whose father had been in business with her own father in Yuhng Keih. Her husband's family was from Fung Lohk Waih in Seiwui, where only major marriage and a kind of minor marriage were practiced. The informant explained that she had, therefore, married without delayed transfer. She said that when a bride in Fung Lohk Waih visited her natal home on the third day after marriage, she was expected to return to her husband's family on the very same day.

The status of delayed transfer marriage within administrative centers, with resident populations of government officials and other representatives of the major-marriage system, is, of course, intriguing. The evidence, though limited, suggests that Canton, the administrative seat of Kwangtung province, presented a mix of marriage systems. Only two of my informants came from the immediate suburbs of Canton, one from Hoh Naahm to the south and the other from Siu Bak to the northeast. According to their accounts, delayed transfer was practiced in those two suburbs, but most informants' accounts suggest that major marriage predominated in Canton. Informants reported that as a general rule, brides from the delayed transfer area who married into Canton and brides from Canton who married into the delayed transfer area married without delayed transfer. On the face of it, therefore, informants' accounts suggest that most residents of Canton practiced major marriage. However, one other factor must figure in an assessment of the status of delayed transfer marriage in Canton. Many of the marriages between Canton and outlying villages were reportedly secondary marriages, which even in the delayed transfer marriage system entailed no delayed transfer.

———

One informant, from Jung Chyun in Punyu county, explained that there were basically three ways in which a man from the delayed transfer marriage area could find a wife who would immediately settle in the husband's home [*jikhaak lohk ga*]. He could take a muijai for a wife. He could marry an adopted daughter (who was usually originally acquired as a muijai). Or, he could go to Canton and find a wife.

———

One informant described the status of delayed transfer marriage in an administrative post near Canton, outside Wohng Bou in Punyu.

———

The informant reported that her village, San Jau Heui, was primarily composed of families of four different surnames and many government officials. Land was devoted to the cultivation of litchi and other fruit. Most men did not work the land themselves but hired workers from nearby villages, and even from Dunggun county. Many villagers left San Jau Heui for Canton and Hong Kong. The informant's father was a very wealthy man who had eleven wives. He owned several thousand *mauh* of land, 24 water buffalo, and employed more than 40 workers. By custom, women in the village married with delayed transfer, and the informant had married in this way. The informant explained that because many girls in the village received an education, age at marriage was late (around 20) and periods of postmarital separation were short, that is, less than three years. She said that some women who married to other villages in Punyu where there was no delayed transfer settled in their husband's home even more quickly [*hou faai lohk ga*], and some even had to settle at once [*jikhaak lohk ga*].

———

Although this informant attributed the short period of nato-local residence in San Jau Heui to the education of girls, the interval of postmarital natolocal residence was undoubtedly influenced by the presence of government officials, representatives of both the Chinese political system and the major-marriage system that it endorsed. Large resident populations of government officials in administrative centers may have profoundly depressed the incidence of delayed transfer marriage. Evidence indicates that the delayed transfer marriage system was subject to political repression by the Ch'ing, Republican, and People's Republic governments.

CH'ING PERCEPTIONS AND REPRESSIONS

Official local histories—county gazetteers—of the Ch'ing period have not proved a rich source for information on delayed transfer marriage.* In principle, the Customs (*Feng-su*) section of those gazetteers should have described an unusual local marriage practice. In the case of another unorthodox form of marriage, minor marriage, the Customs sections provided little information. Arthur Wolf and Chieh-shan Huang attribute this rarity of mentions to efforts at local history that were "largely inspired by hometown chauvinism" (1980, 4; see also 390, *n*10). In the case of delayed transfer marriage, local gentry authors would have been unlikely to comment on an unorthodox practice that would trigger official repression; local magistrates (who were always recruited from outside the area to which they were posted) would have been equally disinclined to draw attention to a practice for which they would be held ultimately responsible. In point of fact, of the few gazetteers that even mention delayed transfer marriage, most portray it as a marriage-resistance phenomenon in which wives refuse to cohabit with husbands. In this interpretation, wives who live apart from their husband are women who are opposed to marriage and who,

*See Appendix D for a list of gazetteers consulted.

when forced to marry, refuse to cohabit. According to the 1853 edition of the Sundak county gazetteer: "Girls in the county form very close relationships with one another and like to make vows of sisterhood with others of the same village. They don't want to marry, and if forced to marry, they stay in their own families, where they enjoy few restrictions. They don't want to return to the husband's family, and some, if forced to return, commit suicide by drowning or hanging."*

What might account for this distorted portrayal of delayed transfer marriage in official accounts of local marriage practices? One possibility is that the cultural prejudices of administrators, members of the major-marriage system, caused them to perceive delayed transfer marriage as a marriage-resistance phenomenon. Judged from the standards of the major-marriage system, wives who were not cohabiting with their husbands may well have been perceived as wives who *refused* to cohabit.

Although cultural prejudice may be partly responsible for this portrayal, another explanation is suggested by an account by Theos. Sampson of Ch'ing political repression. In the September 1868 edition of *Notes and Queries on China and Japan*, Sampson—in response to a query about "anti-marriage associations"—reported that these associations, found in Sundak and Naahmhoi counties, are composed of four to ten girls who live together, presided over by a widow:

A number of young girls agree together that they will not marry, or rather that though the ceremony of marriage may be performed, they will not live with their husbands, either during their whole lives or until all of them have married, and all consent to break up the association; an association loosely formed by young and inexperienced girls might naturally be expected to contain in itself the elements of dissolution, and so in fact members frequently break off from their engagements

*See the Customs (*Feng-su*) section of the 1853 edition of the *Gazetteer of Sundak County* (*Shun-te hsien-chih*). The text that I quote also appears in the Customs section of the 1856 edition of the *Gazetteer of Sundak County*, with the additional comment that although the old customs persisted in poor villages, the situation was improving. For other examples of marriage-resistance portrayals, see the Customs section of the 1871 *Gazetteer of Punyu County* and the 1827 *Gazetteer of Hsiang-shan* [Jungsaan] *County*.

with their associates, to perform the more solemn duties which ripened age demands of them; indeed that men marry girls belonging to these associations betrays a common expectation that the vows of celibacy which they have taken will soon be broken. But in many cases the members of the association remain firm in their resolutions, and the husband, tired of waiting and beginning to despair of ever receiving his wife under his own roof, except on formal ceremonial occasions perhaps, will besiege her parents with complaints, *and sometimes resort to threats and actual violence, or appeals to the magistracy.* . . . Probably it is to the disturbances to which these associations in various ways give rise, that we should attribute the fact that they have been officially denounced and at different times partially put a stop to by the magistrates. (Sampson 1868, 143; my italics)

Perhaps in addition to cultural bias in reporting, the misrepresentation of delayed transfer marriage as marriage resistance is attributable to the way in which delayed transfer marriages came to official attention as *legal cases* in which families disputed the timing of a bridedaughter's assumption of virilocal residence. In the mid-nineteenth century, the customary period of natolocal residence for bridedaughters was reportedly three years (Gray 1878, 1:207–8). When natolocal residence was extended beyond that customary three-year period—when a bridedaughter refused to visit or settle in her husband's family—then conflict erupted between her family and her husband's. This kind of conflict has already been described for a later period, when bridedaughters intent on compensation refused to visit or assume residence with their husband. Nineteenth-century families confronted by bridedaughters reluctant to settle with them resorted to complaints and threats, and ultimately to appeals to local magistrates. As suggested by Sampson and others, these disturbances triggered political repression of local marriage practices (see also Gray 1878, 1:208; Burkhardt 1953–58, 1:108).

A case reading of local marriage practices would therefore lead to a distorted perception of delayed transfer marriage, one in which a wife living apart from her husband appeared to be resisting marriage. Thus, another explanation of the standard nineteenth-century portrayal of delayed transfer marriage is that these marriages were viewed through the distorting medium of legal disputes and were consequently seen as irregular and even dangerous because they appeared to disrupt the social order. Contributing further to the perception of delayed transfer marriage as dangerous were the suicides of bridedaughters who took their lives rather than live with their husband. One case, in which a bridedaughter poisoned herself on the occasion of a conjugal visit, is cited in Chapter 3. That officials saw a connection between the practice of the to them unorthodox delayed transfer form of marriage and suicide among young women is documented in the biographies of two eminent men, whose reputations rested to some extent on their success in suppressing that marriage practice.

The first biography is recorded in the 1910 edition of the *Gazetteer of Naahmhoi County*.* Feng Ju-t'ang, a member of one of the most powerful gentry families in the town of Gau Gong in Naahmhoi, was a scholar whose aspirations for a government position were dashed when he failed to pass the national examinations in 1830. He was, however, awarded a honorary title in 1854 for his role in organizing local militia to suppress the Taiping Rebellion. Although he held no official position, Feng wielded considerable power in Gau Gong, where he used his influence to purge his community of what he felt were undesirable practices, including gambling, prostitution, and delayed transfer marriage. According to a commentary written in the late nineteenth century after Feng's death at the age of 88, there was a custom of long standing in Sundak county and neighboring areas that defied the teachings of Confucius. According to this custom, it was considered "a great shame" for a bride to settle in her husband's home immediately after marriage.† If a bride was

---

*This case appeared in a much abbreviated form in Hsiao Kung-chuan's *Rural China* (1960, 293). The account provided here is based on the biography of Feng Ju-tang in the 1910 edition of the *Gazetteer of Naahmhoi County* (*Nan-hai hsien-chih*) and the commentary that follows it.

†This description of delayed transfer marriage from a commentary following Feng's biography in the 1910 *Gazetteer of Naahmhoi County* together with Li Yün's biography in the 1853 *Gazetteer of Sundak County* (see below) more accurately conveys the customary nature of that marriage system than any other gazetteer account yet found. See 15:1b–2a; 21:31–32.

forced to settle with her husband, she sometimes took her life in revenge, and her family sued for compensation. There were many lawsuits in Gau Gong as a result of these suicides, and many bankruptcies as a result of these suits. According to his biography, Feng, angry about the suicides and bankruptcies, saw the bride's family as frequently exploiting the situation to its financial benefit. In his campaign to suppress delayed transfer marriage, Feng made it known that if a wife committed suicide in her husband's home, his family could deny her proper burial rites—only covering her corpse in straw—and her natal family could not intervene. According to Feng's biographer, as a result of such measures, this marriage practice disappeared.

The second case, which also supports the perceived link between delayed transfer and the suicide of young women, is taken from a biography included in the 1853 edition of the Sundak county gazetteer.* Li Yün, a native of Chekiang province, was posted to Sundak as magistrate in 1818; on his arrival he found that his predecessors had been extremely inefficient in expediting cases brought before the yamen. While clearing up the backlog of cases, Li Yün let it be known that he would promptly consider the cases brought before him by the local people. One day a mother-in-law came to the yamen wanting to sue her daughter-in-law, who wouldn't settle in her husband's home. According to his biography, Li Yün's first reaction was that the suit was a joke; he laughed and dismissed the case. Later he talked to a member of the local gentry and learned about the custom of delayed transfer marriage.

According to Li Yün's biography, this marriage practice was a very old Sundak custom. Before marriage, local girls liked to group together, and once married they saw the husband as the enemy. A few days after marriage, a wife returned to her natal family, visiting her husband's family only on festival occasions. During those visits, a wife ate only food that was prepared by her mother and brought from her natal home. If she was forced to eat anything else, she would threaten suicide. Families wor-

*The biography was referenced by Liang Shao-jen (1837: 4.20a), cited by Topley in an unpublished article (1973, 2).

ried about the possibility of a wife's suicide and the legal troubles it would bring, and therefore let her have her way. It was only after three to four years of marriage—or if she got pregnant—that a wife behaved in the proper way and settled in her husband's home.

After Li Yün learned about delayed transfer marriage, he devised a plan to put a stop to it. From then on, when a mother-in-law came to the yamen to sue her daughter-in-law, Li Yün issued an order for the arrest of the daughter-in-law's father and brothers, whose faces he smeared with black ink to humiliate them. According to his biography, Li Yün was fair and did not excuse a daughter-in-law's family because they were wealthy, but punished rich and poor alike. The local people were shocked by these measures. When a wife's family came to bring suit because of their daughter's suicide, Li Yün ordered them to bury her immediately and dismissed the case. In this way, women came to learn they could bring no advantage to their family by committing suicide. For the next thirty years no further cases of wives' committing suicide occurred, and this was credited to Li Yün. Li Yün's biography was written primarily to document his effectiveness in suppressing this bad marriage practice.

Thus, both suicides and legal disputes triggered the political repression of delayed transfer marriage. In addition, both kinds of incidents contributed to the portrayal of delayed transfer marriage as a marriage-resistance phenomenon.

The portrayal of delayed transfer marriage as marriage resistance continued into the twentieth century. One of the most extreme examples appeared in the *Hongkong Daily Press* in 1900:

There is a peculiar custom in the village of Tai Leong [Daaih Leuhng] and other villages in Shun Tak [Sundak] (Kwong Tung), which may be well characterised as misanthropical, and is highly deprecated even among the natives. Nearly all the girls there have a habit of swearing sisterhood to each other and taking vows of celibacy, looking upon their future husbands as enemies. On the third morning of the wedding, which is generally contracted by their parents, they go home, and refuse to return to their husbands again. Some of them will rather pay money to buy concubines, and others, who are poor and cannot afford to do so, prepare to die together by poison, by throwing themselves into the river, by cutting their throats, or by hanging themselves, so as to be free from the thraldom of their lords. (Quoted in Ball 1901, 6)

A decade later the sociologist Edward Alsworth Ross offered a similar portrayal in *The Changing Chinese*.

In three districts in central Kuangtung, where a girl can always get work at silk-winding, thousands of girls have formed themselves into anti-matrimonial associations, the members of which refuse to live with the husband more than the customary three days. Then they take advantage of their legal right "to visit mother" and never return save on certain days or after a term of years. If the parents attempt to restore the runaway bride to her husband she drowns herself or takes opium; so parents and magistrates have had to let the girls have their way. By presenting herself in her husband's home on certain festival days the bride keeps her wifely status, and if her spouse takes to himself a more tractable mate, she becomes the "number one" wife, and the mistress of the other. (Ross 1911, 204)

The resistance portrayal has continued to be persuasive, no doubt because delayed transfer marriage continues to be measured against the standards of major marriage, and nineteenth-century accounts continue to be quoted as unbiased sources. One additional development has unfortunately reinforced this interpretation. With the popularity in the late nineteenth and early twentieth centuries of compensation marriage—which was in fact a marriage-resistance practice—customary delayed transfer marriage and compensation marriage naturally became mixed in observers' perceptions and portrayals. This is well illustrated in both the *Hongkong Daily Press* article and the excerpt from *The Changing Chinese* quoted above (for further examples, see Hu 1936, 7:27).

Of the nineteenth-century accounts, John Henry Gray's description of delayed transfer marriage is one of the freest from distortion. A longtime resident of Canton, Gray gave an account that accurately conveys the customary nature of this marriage system: "In many districts of the province of Canton, the bride and bridegroom separate at once after the marriage ceremony has been performed. So soon as the festivities are brought to a close, the bride returns to her father's house, there to await the completion of the period of time—generally three years—which it is thought should elapse before the bridal pair are permitted to live together" (1878, 1:207–8).

TWENTIETH-CENTURY PERCEPTIONS AND REPRESSIONS

Only a few modern authors have recognized the customary nature of delayed transfer marriage in the Canton Delta. In an article on local marriage customs, Tien Tsung attempts "to disentangle several customs which have become confused in the minds of those who have heard about them" (1952, 43). He briefly describes the various local marriage practices, differentiating customary marriage with delayed transfer both from a variation and from nonmarriage—that is, from compensation marriage and sworn spinsterhood (1952, 42–43).

One of the best twentieth-century portrayals of the delayed transfer marriage system was provided by K'ai Shih, in a 1926 article in the Chinese journal *New Woman* (*Hsin nü-hsing*). The author describes the practice of delayed transfer marriage in Goumihng county and documents its political repression under the Republican government by reprinting the regulations of the Custom Reform Association of Goumihng (1926, 939–41). The primary purpose of that association was to reform delayed transfer marriage, in effect to Confucianize it. Under the regulations, field investigators were sent to explain to women that they must assume residence with their husband at the proper time, that is, immediately after making the traditional visit home on the third day after marriage. The field investigators were instructed to maintain surveillance over women's marital behavior and report those women who continued to live in their natal home. A married woman who persisted in living at home was persuaded to leave and settle in her husband's family by, among other measures, letters, threats, and fines. If these measures did not induce compliance, the woman's father and brothers were taken before the local authorities. The regulations emphasize that enforcement efforts should focus on the woman and her natal family—and not on her husband's family—in an effort to avoid initiating hostilities between the two families.

So far as I know, there is no written account of the status of delayed transfer marriage under the Japanese occupation (1938–45). A few of my informants reported that during the war with Japan, marriage with delayed transfer ceased. Unfortunately, I could not follow up these reports and therefore do not know how widespread this disruption of the customary marriage system may have been. Moreover, I do not yet know whether this disruption was a general consequence of the social dislocations and political instability of that period or the result of particular policies of the occupying Japanese.

Certainly the most intriguing question is the status of delayed transfer marriage since the establishment of the People's Republic in 1949. By the socialist standards of the new regime, delayed transfer marriage is no more the ideal marriage form than it was for the earlier Confucianists. Marriage, including the question of postmarital residence, has been the target of socialist reform throughout China. Based on his experiences in helping to promulgate the Marriage Law of 1950, the Chinese anthropologist Lin Hui-hsiang—in an article recently brought to my attention—describes delayed transfer marriage as practiced in Hui-an county in Fukien province in 1951.* Unfortunately, he does not give information on the local campaign to implement the Marriage Law or on the specific measures taken to reform delayed transfer marriage. Since the article describes the situation in 1951, he could not as yet discuss the success of the reform

*While still conducting fieldwork, I learned from Eberhard, in a passing reference (1968), and from Tsao, in an article providing only an anecdotal account (1929), that delayed transfer marriage was also practiced in Hui-an county. I am grateful to Zumou Yue and Helen Siu for introducing me to Lin's work, which provides a substantive account of the practice of delayed transfer marriage in Hui-an.

One of China's most renowned anthropologists, Lin Hui-hsiang was a pioneer in the ethnology and archaeology of southeast China. Born in Taiwan in 1901, Lin graduated from the Department of Sociology at Hsia-men (Amoy) University in 1926, and at the time of his death in 1958 was professor and chair of the Department of History at Hsia-men, director of the Institute of Southeast Asian Studies, and curator of the Museum of Anthropology at Hsia-men.

efforts. Lin's article does provide, however, a relatively recent account of the delayed transfer marriage system in Chinese society. Although I briefly compare the practice of delayed transfer in Kwangtung and Fukien in the Conclusion, several points are relevant to the present discussion.

As in the Canton Delta, brides in delayed transfer marriages in Hui-an separated from their husbands three days after marriage and returned to live in their natal home for at least two to three years, and often for longer. Bridedaughters were expected to visit their husband's home on the occasion of several festivals each year and settled there permanently on first pregnancy. Again as in the Canton Delta, delayed transfer marriage became the target of government reform because it was perceived as contributing to high rates of female suicide. Even with incomplete statistics, Lin reports 122 female suicides for Hui-an county between October 1949 and August 1950. Some suicides were individual, others collective. Lin attributed female suicides in Hui-an to the liminal position of bridedaughters, who were neither residents in their husband's home nor permanent residents in their own natal home. He saw bridedaughters as torn between two families, especially when they developed affection for their husband, which they were forced to conceal or be ridiculed by their "sisters." Still another reason for the unhappiness of bridedaughters was their double work load. In Hui-an, an agricultural area, bridedaughters were expected to contribute labor at harvest times to both their husband's family and their own family. Since they returned to their own home in the evening after working at their husband's home—sometimes traveling a considerable distance to do so—bridedaughters suffered from (and complained bitterly about) extreme exhaustion (Lin 1981, 255–58).

Thus, Lin attributed the high incidence of female suicide in Hui-an to what he perceived as the generally unhappy lot of bridedaughters in delayed transfer marriages. We are not given sufficient information, however, to place the incidence of female suicide in historical and cultural perspective. We do not know the effect of the tremendous social dislocations of the preceding two decades—including civil war—on the marriage system and life in general in Hui-an county. Furthermore, was the reported double labor contribution a practice of long standing or of more recent introduction? Unfortunately, given the sparse data, we can conclude only that delayed transfer marriage once again became the object of government repression in part because it was associated with female suicide.

Lin also provided evidence that, as in the Canton Delta, disputes over the interval of separation in delayed transfer marriages could escalate to become legal cases, which may also have stimulated official repression. In one contemporary case reported by Lin, a bridedaughter who had been married for five to six years refused to visit her husband. News that the husband had begun to look for another wife reached the bridedaughter's family, and in the quarrel that ensued, relatives of the bride struck the husband's mother. The husband then joined the army. When the government started divorce proceedings, however, the bridedaughter relented and settled in her husband's home (Lin 1981, 255).

The full story of the efforts in the Canton Delta to reform delayed transfer marriage has yet to be learned. I have heard reports that early post-Liberation attempts to restore bridedaughters and spinsters to their "proper" home resulted in a rash of suicides. During interviews in 1986, when I pressed for a more contemporary account of delayed transfer marriage, several informants who had recently visited their home villages in the Canton Delta reported that marriage with delayed transfer was re-emerging in some places. Intervals of postmarital separation are reportedly much shorter now than before. For example, an informant from Lahk Lauh in Sundak county reported that before the Liberation a bride lived apart from her husband for seven to eight years, but now couples remained separated for only two to three months or at most for one to two years. Of course, the as-yet-unanswered questions are where, to what extent, and under what conditions is delayed transfer marriage re-emerging?

During a special tour through the sericultural area of the

Canton Delta in the summer of 1986, my assistant and I attempted to discuss delayed transfer marriage with the local official acting as our guide. Unfortunately, we were unable to learn more of contemporary marriage practices, but we did learn more about spinster houses. According to the official, although spinster houses per se no longer exist in Sundak, the government has opened retirement homes in small villages for old women who used to be sworn spinsters. The government has even hired people to cook for them. The official said the old women can stay in these homes until they die; because of an old custom, they cannot die at home, she said. When a spinster dies, her tablet can be placed in one of these government-run houses, which are known by such names as Respecting the Elders House.*

The recent official recognition—and even respect—given sworn spinsters reflects an ideological re-evaluation of the position of these women in local history. According to a recent Chinese publication, *A Look at Sundak* (*Shun-te feng-mao*), sworn spinsterhood is now perceived in part as the rebellion of local women against their oppression under the feudal family system (1985, 118–19).

Although a complete account of its status in contemporary China has yet to be given, delayed transfer marriage has since at least the early nineteenth century been subject to political repression, partly because of distorted perceptions of what it involved. The causes of this distortion, manifest in the portrayal of delayed transfer marriage as marriage resistance, were the cultural bias of members of the major-marriage system and an interpretation of local marriage custom based on suicides and legal cases. Also contributing to this portrayal was a vigorous antimarital bias among young women in some villages in the nineteenth century, a subject to which I now turn.

---

*See Parish and Whyte for a description of girls' houses in Canton Delta villages in the 1970's (1978, 208, 231–32). See also Chan et al. for an account of how a widow who ran a girls' house in a Delta village during the 1970's was accused of telling her charges "salacious tales" and "old vulgar stories" (1984, 164–65).

7

Anti-marital Bias
and the Rise of
Marriage Alternatives

Standard nineteenth-century portrayals of marriage customs in the Canton Delta typically appear in conjunction with reports of a vigorous anti-marital bias, manifest among unmarried girls in vows never to marry, among bridedaughters in declarations never to return to their husband, and in both groups in threats of suicide if forced to marry or to rejoin their husband. Anti-marital bias among young women figured significantly not only in extending the periods of natolocal residence in delayed transfer marriages in the nineteenth century, but also in the rise of marriage-resistance practices. The data suggest that those practices—compensation marriage, sworn spinsterhood, and bride-initiated spirit marriage—flourished in a temporal sequence. Several basic relationships can be established. First, the rise of an anti-marital bias among young women preceded—and was a necessary social precondition for—the rise of alternatives to delayed transfer marriage, that is, to marriage resistance. Second, the mechanization of sericulture and the subsequent employment of women as silk reelers in steam filatures provided the economic basis for the rise of alternatives to marriage. Third, the heyday of compensation marriage preceded the rise of sworn spinsterhood. Fourth, as demonstrated in Chapter 5, bride-initiated spirit marriage was at its height during the earliest generation of spinsterhood.

SUICIDE, WITCHCRAFT, AND SISTERHOODS

The best evidence for the anti-marital bias in villages practicing delayed transfer marriage in the nineteenth century comes from accounts of female suicide, which also illuminate the distinctive tensions within delayed transfer marriages. In Taiwan, the incidence of female suicide has been shown to be highest during the early years of marriage and virilocal residence, typically a stressful period for young women in the major-marriage system (M. Wolf 1975, 121–24). In the delayed transfer marriage system, female suicides also occurred frequently early in the marriage process. For example, a suicide during a conjugal visit is described by John Henry Gray in an account cited in Chapter 3. In addition, a marked incidence of suicide at the time wives settled with husbands is documented in the Customs section of the 1853 edition of the Sundak county gazetteer, in the biography of Li Yün in that same gazetteer, and in the biography of Feng Ju-t'ang (?1800–1890) in the 1910 edition of the Naahmhoi county gazetteer. But the specific timing of these suicides—on the occasion of the engagement or marriage rites, at the point of transfer to the husband's home, or during a conjugal visit—suggests the involvement of something more than strained relations between a young woman and her affines.

One variety of female suicide provides strong evidence of an anti-marital bias among young women. Suicides occurring in the *natal* village before marriage or before the assumption of permanent residence in the husband's home gained special notoriety in the nineteenth century because they sometimes entailed the collective suicide of several young women.

An early reference to collective suicide appeared in the *Chinese Repository* (1833–34, 190). A young bride returning from her husband's house "according to established custom" gave her friends and sisters a shocking account of marriage. Four of the girls, "alleging that it was better to die than go to the house of a bad man," then committed suicide by tying their hands together and throwing themselves into a river twenty miles west of Canton.

John Henry Gray provided two of the most informative accounts of collective suicide.

During the reign of Taou-Kwang [1821–50], fifteen virgins whom their parents had affianced, met together upon learning the fact, and resolved to commit suicide. They flung themselves into a tributary stream of the Canton river, in the vicinity of the village where they lived. The tomb in which the corpses were interred near Fo-chune [Fo Chyun] is called the Tomb of the Virgins.

     . . . . .

At a village near Whampoa called Siu-tong-ki in July 1873, eight young girls, who had been affianced, drowned themselves in order to avoid marriage. They clothed themselves in their best attire, and at eleven o'clock, in the darkness of night, the eight maidens, who had bound themselves together, threw themselves into a tributary of the Canton river. (Gray 1878, 1:185–86)

Other references to collective suicide can be found in J. Dyer Ball (1901, 6), Edward Alsworth Ross (1911, 204), the Customs section of the Punyu county gazetteer (1871), S. H. Peplow and M. Barker (1931, 117), and the quotation from *Hongkong Daily Press* cited in Chapter 6. Arthur Smith gave this account, translated from an article in the Chinese newspaper *Shih Pao*, entitled "Suicide as Virtue."

There is a prevailing custom in a district called Shun-te [Sundak] in the Canton province, among female society to form different kinds of sisterhoods such as "All pure" sisterhoods, "Never-to-be-married" sisterhoods, etc. Each sisterhood consists of about ten young maidens who swear vows to heaven never to get married, as they regard marriages as something horrid, believing that their married lives would be miserable and unholy; and their parents fail to prevail upon them to yield.

A sad case has just happened: a band of young maidens ended their existence in this world by drowning themselves in the Dragon River because one of them was forced by her parents to be married. She was engaged in her childhood before she joined this sisterhood. When her parents had made all the necessary arrangements for her marriage she reported the affair to the other members of her sisterhood who at once agreed to die for her cause, if she remained constant to her sworn vows to be single and virtuous. Should she violate the laws of the sisterhood and yield to her parents, her life was to be taunted as a worthless being. She consulted with them as to the best mode of escaping this marriage, and they all agreed to die with her, if she could plan to run away from her parents on the night of the marriage.

As there were many friends to watch her movements, it was almost impossible for her to escape, so she attempted her life by swallowing a gold ring, but any serious consequence that might have resulted was prevented by the administration of a powerful emetic. She was finally taken by force and made over to the male side, to her great grief. According to the usual custom she was allowed to return to her parents. During all this time she was planning a way to escape to her sisters. By bribing the female servants she was taken one night to her sisters under the cover of darkness. The sisters at once joined with her in terminating their lives by jumping into the Dragon River with its swift currents, which rapidly carried them off. (Smith 1899, 287)

Of course, these accounts can tell us nothing about the frequency of collective suicide in the nineteenth century, and a few notorious cases were cited again and again.* What these accounts do confirm, however, is that the girls' house played an important role in the socialization of women and the rise of a vigorous anti-marital bias in some places. The imprint of the girls' house can be seen in all the foregoing accounts of collective suicide; these accounts suggest that collective suicide involved members of the same girls' house. As noted in Chapter 2, the girls' house provided the opportunity for a group of girls to hear shocking tales of marriage from a returned bride or bride-daughter. In addition, in fostering close relations among girls— who were agemates and often lineage kinswomen—the girls' house was the natural setting for the generation of the vows and

---

*Tien is convinced that most Sundak people have one particular case in mind when they speak of collective suicide, the celebrated case of the "six girls jumping in the river" (1952, 41). Ball also refers to this one famous incident (1901, 6).

associations that were popular among young women of the area. The girls' house provided the opportunity to organize efforts to resist marriage and lent a measure of persuasion to suicide threats. Furthermore, the girls' house, as a designated sleeping quarters, provided girls with the opportunity to group together at night, and to steal away unnoticed.

Other evidence of an anti-marital bias in the nineteenth century is provided by reports of witchcraft directed against husbands. Nicholas B. Dennys, an editor of the *China Review*, recorded the following incident in his book, *The Folklore of China*.

It used to be believed at Canton, and perhaps now is, that the blood of an unborn infant was all-effective for magical purposes. It is used as a charm against husbands by a sect called [*mai fu gaau*], a set of young unmarried women, comprising a sisterhood who are sworn never to marry. If forced to do so, they then employ this charm to destroy their husbands in order to remain single, and be faithful to the oaths of the sisterhood. (Dennys 1876, 68)

Unfortunately, none of my informants recognized this so-called *mai fu gaau* sect. However, John Henry Gray also described a *mai fu gaau* sect, located it within the delayed transfer marriage area in the Sai Tiuh area of Naahmhoi county and in Sundak, and demonstrated that it was locally credited with a certain measure of success.

In the district of Shun-tuk [Sundak], and at Si-chu-shan [Sai Tiuh], a portion of the district of Nam-hoi in Kwang-tung, there are women called Mi-Foo-Kow, who profess by incantations and other mysterious means to be able to effect the death of their fellow-creatures. They are consulted by married women who being cruelly treated, or for other reasons, are anxious secretly to kill their husbands. The witches gather the bones of infants from the public cemeteries, and invoke the evil genii of the infants to accompany them to their dwelling-houses. The bones are reduced to a fine powder, and sold in this form. Mixed in tea, wine, or any other beverage, the powder is daily given to her husband by the murderous wife. At the same time the witch daily calls upon the evil genius of the infant whose bones have been used to assist in effecting the death of the object of the woman's hate. Sometimes, in addition to this horrible daily draught, a portion of the bone of an infant is carefully secreted under his bed. Attempts have been made, I believe, not without success, to destroy these witches. In the Toong-Yan-Shan-Hok, or public hall at Kang-hee, near to Si-chu-shan, some of these women were summoned into the presence of the gentry, and made to answer certain grave charges of this nature which had been preferred against them by their neighbours. Upon being convicted, they were put to death by poison. Not later than the year 1865, several women of this class were put to death in this manner. (Gray 1878, 2:24)

Another reference to *mai fu gaau* practitioners can be found in J. Dyer Ball (1901, 7). In addition, B. C. Henry seems to implicate an "anti-matrimonial league" in Naahmhoi Sai Tiuh in the practice of witchcraft.

The existence of this Amazonian league has long been known, but as to its rules and the number of its members no definite information has come to hand. It is comprised of young widows and marriageable girls. Dark hints are given as to the methods used to escape matrimony. The sudden demise of betrothed husbands, or the abrupt ending of the newly-married husband's career, suggest unlawful means for dissolving the bonds. (Henry 1886, 69)

In spite of young women's protests, vows never to marry, and suicide threats, the sources report that women were in due course compelled to marry and eventually to return to their husband. The reconciliation of these positions seems best addressed by Theos. Sampson, who observed that the organization of young women to protest marriage contained in itself elements of dissolution, and "indeed that men marry girls belonging to these associations betrays a common expectation that the vows of celibacy which they have taken will soon be broken" (1868, 143).

THE ORIGINS OF COMPENSATION MARRIAGE

It is significant, however, that none of these reports of political repression, suicide, and anti-marital bias in the nineteenth century referred to compensation marriage. Surely such an exotic practice (to both Chinese of the major-marriage system and Westerners) would have received considerable notice. In fact, the standard nineteenth-century interpretation of delayed transfer marriage as a form of marriage resistance would have been reinforced by reports of women compensating husbands. The absence of such reports supports the view, advanced here and in Chapter 8, that compensation marriage as a popular alternative to marriage arose at the end of the nineteenth century. Significantly, by the beginning of the twentieth century, accounts of marriage resistance do include features that are clearly descriptive of compensation marriage. One early example is the article from the *Hongkong Daily Press* in 1900, quoted in Chapter 6.

Even the best nineteenth-century observer, John Henry Gray, made no reference to compensation marriage. Gray's most complete statement on anti-marital bias among women cited two other alternatives to marriage, but not compensation marriage: "In one street alone—the Shap-bat-kan street in the Honam suburb of Canton—I knew four families in which there were ladies who positively refused to marry, upon the ground that, should their husbands become polygamists, there would remain for them a life of unhappiness. To avoid marriage some become Buddhist or Taouist nuns; and others prefer death itself to marriage" (1878, 1:185). Indeed, there were many nunneries in the vicinity of Canton.* However, the fact that the only other alternative Gray described is death itself argues persuasively against the existence of less drastic alternatives such as compensation marriage.

The evidence suggests, then, a lack of popular recourse to compensation marriage before the late nineteenth century. But compensation as a traditional means of renegotiating marriage terms may have antedated that marriage alternative. That is, there may have been a more general precedent for the specialized late-nineteenth-century form of compensation as a means of extending traditional periods of natolocal residence. An intriguing, though ambiguous, report of what may be a precursor

---

*See the Customs (*Feng-su*) sections of the 1871 edition of the *Gazetteer of Punyu County* (*P'an-yü hsien-chih*) and of the 1856 edition of the *Gazetteer of Sundak County* (*Shun-te hsien-chih*).

of compensation marriage is found in the biography of Feng Ju-t'ang and following commentary in the 1910 edition of the Naahmhoi county gazetteer (see Chapter 6). A commentary written after Feng's death in the late nineteenth century and based on interviews with his grandson describes a practice in which some married women returned the bridewealth to their husbands and asked them to find concubines instead. Thereafter, the relationship between husband and wife was reportedly severed. Many such cases occurred in Gau Gong, which angered Feng and further fired his reformist zeal. Was the "bridewealth" in these cases in fact returned—in which event a married woman's parents would have returned it—or was this a misinterpretation of a financial transaction as in compensation marriage? Was the relationship between husband and wife truly severed or was it preserved in altered form as in compensation marriage? Unfortunately, whether this provocative account describes a kind of annulment or some early form of a compensation-type arrangement is an open question.

From the literature and from interviews, I have drawn a few examples in which compensation was clearly a general means of renegotiating marriage agreements. In these examples, parents of the bride, subsequent to the arrangement of marriage, sought to cancel the marriage agreement. The first case, from Punyu, was reported in the 1832–33 edition of the *Chinese Repository*.

The bad effects of the system of early betrothing young children, or even infants before they are born, as is sometimes done, was exemplified the other day in a case which occurred in a village of the Paanyu district. The lad Ho was early betrothed to the lass Seay, of course, without their consent. When this took place, both families were prosperous. Ho's affairs, however, went ill in the world, before the proper age for marriage arrived. On this account marriage was deferred for several years, till the lady reached the age of 24, and the gentleman 26. He appears to have been some spoiled child, which Miss Seay would, of course, know by report, though she was supposed never to have seen him. Her family wished to get rid of the contract, but the poor and the profligate would not consent to give up the match. The unfortunate young woman must marry. Therefore, on the 25th day of the 9th moon, the external ceremonies were performed, and the lady was carried to the house of the husband.

When evening came, however, she would not retire; but addressing her husband said, "touch me not, my mind is resolved to abandon the world, and become a nun. I shall this night cut off my hair. I have saved two hundred dollars, which I give to you. With the half you may purchase a concubine; and with the rest enter on some trade. Be not lazy and thriftless. Hereafter remember me." On saying which, she instantly cut off her hair. The kindred, and worthless husband, seeing her resolution, and, of course, fearing suicide, acquiesced, and Miss Seay, who left her father's house to become a wife, returned as a nun. It is said, young ladies are often reduced to this necessity, and cry, and plead with their parents to permit it, rather than become wives of men reduced to poverty, and perhaps of bad character besides. But few have the resolution to get rid of a bad bargain in the spirited manner of Miss Seay. (*Chinese Repository* 1832–33, 293)

Another case demonstrating compensation as a general means of renegotiating marriage contracts is drawn from my own field data on spirit marriage. Although bride-initiated spirit marriage enjoyed a certain popularity among both unmarried girls and spinsters who were in need of a host, one form of spirit marriage was seldom embraced eagerly by young women or their parents. *Sau ching,* in which a woman married the spirit of her deceased fiancé, meant "many restrictions" for the bride. As mentioned earlier, a bride in *sau ching* was required to participate in mourning for her deceased groom, assume immediate virilocal residence, and conduct herself in an exemplary manner for the rest of her life. According to a Sundak informant, parents who did not want their daughter to suffer these restrictions arranged to compensate the parents of the deceased in order to break the marriage agreement.

One other case was described to me by an informant from Naahm Seh Chyun in Dunggun county, outside the delayed transfer marriage area. According to the informant, in her village there was no such thing as wives' paying compensation to the husband's family and negotiating a compensation marriage. But if a girl ran away after her marriage was arranged, then her father had to recompense the groom's family.

These cases suggest that compensation was a traditional means of renegotiating marriage contracts; if so, this has implications for our interpretation of the distinctive marriage form—compensation marriage—that arose in the delayed transfer marriage area. As the special recourse for bridedaughters who wished to extend the customary period of natolocal residence, compensation marriage is perhaps best viewed as the efflorescence and specialization of a traditional and general means of renegotiating marriages to meet the special needs of bridedaughters in the late nineteenth and early twentieth centuries.

On the basis of interview data, compensation marriage can be dated to as early as "mother's generation" for informants aged 85 to 90 in 1980 (born 1890–95), or roughly in the 1890's. Informants of all ages typically described compensation marriage as popular or more common "a generation ago," "among the older ones," "in father's sister's generation," or "in mother's generation." Although retrospective data bearing on practices of an earlier generation must be considered with caution, many informants were able to name specific individuals in those generations who had negotiated compensation marriages (see Chapter 3).

The rise of compensation marriage in its popular guise can probably be established as no earlier than the 1880's. This estimate is based partly on the absence of documentation of that practice in the writings of John Henry Gray for the 1860's and 1870's and in other early accounts. In addition, the effects of the mechanization of silk reeling, the primary source for compensation funds, were not widely felt before the 1880's (see Chapter 8).

COMPENSATION MARRIAGE VERSUS
SWORN SPINSTERHOOD

If the heyday of compensation marriage can be established roughly as beginning around 1890, what can be said about its decline? Interview data demonstrate that compensation marriage preceded the rise of sworn spinsterhood as a popular alternative to marriage. Twenty-four of the 25 informants providing intragenerational comparative data on the incidence of compensation marriage and sworn spinsterhood who reported that spinsterhood was popular in their own generation also reported a lower incidence of compensation marriage for that same generation. Only one very elderly informant, aged 90, reported that compensation marriage was popular in her own generation. Of the 35 informants providing intergenerational comparative data on the incidence of compensation marriage and spinsterhood, 33 informants claimed that the incidence of compensation marriage had been greater in preceding generations. In fact, only the two eldest informants providing intergenerational data (aged 87 and 90) reported that compensation marriage was popular in their own generation.

In general, for informants between the ages of 65 and 80 in 1980 (born 1900–1915), the following configuration of relationships emerges:

	Compensation marriage	Sworn spinsterhood
Mother's generation or earlier	Many	Few
Informant's generation	Few	Many

Informants' accounts suggest that compensation marriage could not compete with sworn spinsterhood as an alternative to customary delayed transfer marriage. Sworn spinsterhood was less expensive—there was no compensation to pay—and it was therefore the logical choice when both alternatives to marriage were available. One 72-year-old informant from Yuhng Keih in Sundak explained the popularity of spinsterhood in her own generation in this way: "If a woman married and didn't settle with her husband, then she had to pay compensation. Wasn't it easier to stay unmarried and become a sworn spinster?"

So great was the popularity of spinsterhood in the informants' own generation that informants from some villages reported that more women became spinsters than brides. The following case describes such a situation and further illustrates the comparative incidence of compensation marriage and spinsterhood.

The 81-year-old informant was from Jung Chyun in Punyu, a rice-producing area. She reported that in her village many women didn't want to marry, and that in her generation spinsterhood was popular. Most spinsters made their own living as domestic servants in Hong Kong. Girls who wanted to become spinsters usually planned to run away when they were 14 or 15 years old. Even if a girl wanted to become a nun, she had to run away, because in her village people didn't like nuns! In her generation, few women married, and most left to become spinsters in Hong Kong. There were some spinsters in mother's generation, but many more in her own. She explained that in mother's generation, girls didn't know how to run away to become spinsters and work as domestic servants in Hong Kong. When they tried to run away, they were captured, brought back to the village, and forced to marry. Later, many of these women compensated their husbands. According to the informant, there were a lot of compensation marriages in mother's generation.

Just as informants typically described spinsterhood as more popular in their own generation, they also described it as less popular in preceding generations. In most accounts, spinsterhood emerges as a more radical practice than compensation marriage. As described earlier, some daughters who wanted to become spinsters were forced by parents to contract spirit marriages instead (see Chapter 5). Others who wanted to become spinsters were forced to marry and later arranged compensation. One Sundak informant explained that there were so few spinsters in her own village in her mother's generation because fathers and uncles were conservative and feared that girls who became sworn spinsters would later marry and ruin the family reputation.

The account of another informant further illustrates the comparative incidence of compensation marriage and spinsterhood and describes yet another constraint on the practice of spinsterhood in "mother's" generation.

An 85-year-old informant from Bak Muhn San Gei, a single-surname village near the silk center of Daaih Leuhng in Sundak, reported that spinsterhood was popular in her generation. The informant is herself a spinster, and like many spinsters in Bak Muhn reeled silk in local steam filatures. Spinsters were not permitted to live at home but were required to live in spinster houses. In contrast to her own generation, all women in mother's generation had to marry and return to live in their husband's home after three years. At that time, there were no silk factories and no spinster houses. Women in mother's generation still had bound feet.

Thus, on the basis of the various comparative data, the heyday of compensation marriage can be established roughly as 1890–1910 and the heyday of sworn spinsterhood as 1910–1930.

THE ORIGINS OF SWORN SPINSTERHOOD

Like compensation marriage, sworn spinsterhood may have been the efflorescence and specialization of a traditional institution, adapted to meet the needs of women in the early twentieth century. The data indicate that in addition to the popular version of spinsterhood—a recourse for women seeking independent careers and way of life—there were other forms of spinsterhood, serving different functions. The comments of a few informants suggested that sworn spinsterhood in its popular version coexisted with, and overshadowed, two other variations of spinsterhood. In contrast to the popular version, these variations of spinsterhood were not radical forms and seemed integrated with traditional social life. The rise of the version popular in the early twentieth century can probably be attributed to a combination of factors, including the changed demands for female labor in the silk industry and a relaxation of normative constraints on the practice of marriage alternatives, in the wake of perhaps two generations of compensation marriages.

In one variation, described by a few informants from within the delayed transfer marriage area, some spinsters from wealthy families were supported by their families. These families provided their spinster daughter with a house and settled on her a share of the family estate, usually a portion equivalent to dowry. This variation of spinsterhood defies the popular image of spinster as an independent daughter, capable of supporting herself and her family. The heiress-spinster undertook no career and made no economic contribution to her family; instead she was entirely dependent on them. In fact, her dependence undoubtedly enhanced the social prestige of her family and lineage by demonstrating their ability to support a daughter over her entire lifespan.

One key informant, in a series of interviews, placed the tradition of heiress-spinster in the broader context of a nonradical tradition of spinsterhood. This account was especially significant because the informant's natal village lay outside the delayed transfer marriage area, in an adjacent part of Jungsaan county, in Hou Tauh near the town of Sehk Keih. (She was the only informant from a major-marriage village who reported a tradition of spinsterhood.)

The informant, a 90-year-old Buddhist nun, the educated daughter of a teacher, was renowned throughout her community for her love for "talking history." She reported that sworn spinsterhood was popular in both Sehk Keih and Hou Tauh. Since this area produced rice and not silk, spinsters in the popular tradition supported themselves as domestic servants in Macau and Hong Kong.

But in addition to the popular version of spinsterhood, the informant also described the heiress-spinster tradition for Sehk Keih and Hou Tauh. The heiress-spinster was completely dependent on her natal family. She was given a house by her family, where she was required to stay at festival times. The heiress-spinster inherited a share of the family estate, and on her own death, left her property and house to an adopted daughter, her apprentice in spinsterhood [touhdai]. If she had no adopted daughter, by tradition her house then became a vegetarian house [chai-t'ang].

The informant described two situations in which a family could "force" their daughter to become a spinster [bik keuih sohei]. [The very idea of being forced brought incredulous looks to the faces of informants from within the delayed transfer area, who protested that whereas women could be forced to marry, they wanted to become spinsters!] The first situation was one in which a family had arranged a marriage for their son but could make no suitable match for his elder sister. The informant explained that parents would then force the elder daughter to become a spinster so that her younger brother could marry. In this way, proper sibling order was observed in the arrangement of marriage. The second situation was one in which a daughter had a history of broken engagements or had a fiancé who had died. When she became older and her marriage prospects bleak, this daughter would be forced by her parents to become a spinster.

The most surprising variation of spinsterhood described by the informant for the Sehk Keih–Hou Tauh area was a tradition by which muijai became spinsters. On reaching marriageable age and on the invitation of her employer, a muijai could choose to become a spinster rather than marry out as a secondary wife. A muijai-spinster continued to serve in the home for the duration of her employer's life. According to the informant, this option of becoming a spinster was available only to "sold" as opposed to "pawned" muijai.

The employer himself hosted the spinster banquet for a muijai when she reached the age of 20. The banquet was held in a vegetarian hall and the muijai's parents were among the invited guests. Everyone gave red envelopes of good luck money [leihsih] to the muijai-spinster, who served tea "as at a marriage banquet," but served her employer first. After the spinster banquet, the muijai-spinster continued in the employer's service, for which she received no wage. The employer provided for her, even giving her clothes. Muijai-spinsters often became close personal maids [*gansan*], responsible for the personal care of family members. They also specialized in arranging the often-elaborate buns worn by married women. The informant said that occasionally a muijai-spinster might be allowed to work outside the employer's home for neighbors, for example, helping to make clothes. In this way she could earn a little money, but she was never permitted to work outside her employer's home for longer than one month. The muijai-spinster might use the money she earned for gifts, but she did not send money home to her parents.

Because the muijai-spinster was raised in the employer's home, her relationship with her employer's family was often quite close. According to the informant, she was treated "like an adopted daughter." When the employer lay dying, he gave instructions to his son to provide the muijai-spinster with enough money so that she could support herself through old age. Or alternatively, the muijai-spinster could choose to continue to serve other family members. The informant explained that the muijai-spinster could not claim money on her employer's death, but she was treated like an adopted daughter and provided for. The employer might even arrange to give a sum of money to a Buddhist temple or nunnery, to which the muijai-spinster could retire when old or dying.

———

Thus, the traditions of heiress-spinster, muijai-spinster, and compensation as a means of renegotiating marriage terms may have been precursors of the later, radical marriage-resistance practices of sworn spinsterhood and compensation marriage. Conceivably, those early traditions were changed and redefined to meet the special needs of women during the late nineteenth and early twentieth centuries. What caused the changes? This chapter has shown that an anti-marital bias flourished among young women in some places in the nineteenth century, as demonstrated by the pattern of female suicides and reports of resistance to both marriage and settling in the husband's home. Anti-marital bias was an important social precondition for the rise of compensation marriage and sworn spinsterhood as popular marriage alternatives. I have also alluded to the significance of economic factors in the rise of the marriage alternatives, in particular to changes associated with the mechanization of sericulture and employment of women as reelers in steam filatures. The next chapter considers these economic changes in more detail.

8

The Link Between Sericulture and Marriage

The preceding chapters have established that the heyday of compensation marriage preceded the rise of sworn spinsterhood and that supplementary bride-initiated spirit marriages characterized the early practice of sworn spinsterhood. In addition, the discussion has also demonstrated the significance of both anti-marital biases among young women and economic opportunities in the rise of marriage alternatives. This chapter seeks to explain the rise of the first alternative to marriage—compensation marriage—which loosened normative constraints and initiated an era of popular marriage alternatives. Why did compensation marriage effloresce in the late nineteenth century?

My research has demonstrated that the practice of compensation marriage was most firmly established in sericultural villages within the delayed transfer marriage area. This chapter argues that through the traditional association of the marital status of bridedaughter with the economic role of silk reeling, delayed transfer marriage and sericulture became functionally linked.

Because of this link, changes in silk reeling as a result of mechanization directly affected the status of bridedaughter, and consequently the practice of customary delayed transfer marriage. Specifically, the high wages and mobility for silk reelers that came with mechanization raised the prestige of bridedaughters within natal families while strengthening their position outside families.

SERICULTURE IN THE DELAYED TRANSFER MARRIAGE AREA

In 1925, C. W. Howard and K. P. Buswell, sericultural experts at Ling Nan Agricultural College in Canton, estimated that Kwangtung province alone produced one-seventh of the world's raw silk (1925, 40). My field research has shown that the heart of the Kwangtung sericultural industry lay wholly within the delayed transfer marriage area and that over half of the delayed transfer marriage area was devoted to sericulture. Map 3 shows the extent of mulberry cultivation in the Canton Delta. Within the four main counties constituting the delayed transfer marriage area, Sundak, Punyu, Naahmhoi, and Jungsaan, more than two million persons were engaged in sericulture in 1925.*

All sericulture within the core area was characterized by the "four-water-six-land" (sei tohng luhk deih) system, unique to the Canton Delta. In this system, Delta lands were systematically diked and raised with earth from the excavation of fish ponds, resulting in a water-to-land ratio of four to six. The four-water-six-land system—also known as "diked mulberry grove fish pond" cultivation (song gei yu tohng)—was organized to yield the greatest productivity from the related enterprises of mulberry cultivation, fish breeding, and silkworm rearing. The diked or raised lands were planted in mulberry, and the excavated ponds became fisheries. Mulberry trees were cultivated for their leaves, the exclusive diet of the silkworms. Silkworm waste was used to

---

*This figure is based on estimates by Howard and Buswell of the number of persons engaged in sericulture in each of the four counties: 200,000 in Naahmhoi, 382,600 in Jungsaan, 1,440,000 in Sundak, 15,000 in Punyu (1925, 15–25).

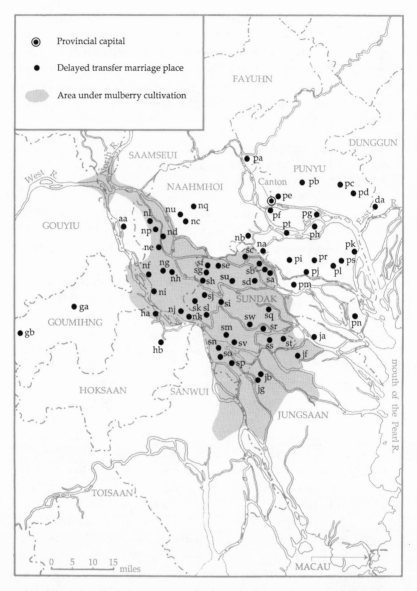

Map 3: Delayed transfer marriage and sericulture. See Appendix C for place-name identification.

feed the fish. At the end of the year, the fish were sold, and the ponds drained. Fish waste and the silt at the bottom of ponds were excavated and applied as fertilizer at the base of mulberry trees. Thus, a close relationship existed between mulberry cultivation, silkworm raising, and fish breeding, which was popularly expressed as "strong worms, fat fish, prosperous mulberry fields; fertile ponds, abundant leaves, and strong cocoons" (FSTC* 1976, 4:57; Chung 1958, 259, 263, 1980, 200–202; Miao and Ch'en 1966, 78–79; Chou 1987, 69).

In areas where the diked mulberry groves and fish ponds were established earliest—in Gau Gong in Naahmhoi, Luhng Saan and Luhng Gong in Sundak, and Siu Laahm in Jungsaan—this system was still further developed by the end of the nineteenth century to include pig raising. Lotus plants, grown on the surface of ponds, were used to feed the pigs, and pig waste was used both to fertilize mulberry groves and to feed the fish (FSTC 1976, 4:58; Chung 1980, 200, 207).

The four-water-six-land system of sericulture developed out of efforts over the last thousand years to raise the level of Delta lands and control flooding. The reclaimed, raised areas were originally planted in fruit trees and the system was known as "diked fruit orchard fish pond" cultivation (*gwo gei yu tohng*). Although sericulture had long been practiced in the Delta, it was not until after the beginning of the sixteenth century that fruit orchards were systematically replaced with mulberry groves in the diked areas. A fixed proportion of water to land developed in those diked areas, representing the optimal ratio for greatest silk production. By the early seventeenth century in Gau Gong in Naahmhoi, one of the earliest places in which the diked mulberry grove fish pond system was established, the proportion of water to land varied from three:seven to four:six. By the end of the nineteenth century, however, diked mulberry grove

* Although some scholars might question the reliability of a work compiled during the Cultural Revolution, I cite FSTC both because its primary sources for the discussion of the development of the silk industry are reports by K'ao Huo (1925) and Liu Po-yüan (1922) and because recent works by reputable scholars, including those of Chung Kung-fu (1980) and Ssu-t'u (1986), also cite it.

fish pond lands in Gau Gong and elsewhere were typically established in the four-water-six-land proportion (Chung 1958, 263, 265, 1980, 200; Ssu-t'u 1986, 108).

The organization of sericultural lands in the four:six system facilitated the further intensification of an already labor-intensive industry. In Sundak county—virtually wholly contained within the sericultural area (and within the delayed transfer marriage area)—70 percent of the land was devoted to sericulture and 80 percent of the population engaged in that industry.

The estimates on population engaged in sericulture vary with the place reported, villages give 10% or more, country areas 90% or more, but the average for the entire district would be at least 80%. As one goes about the district it seems that aside from the necessary business to supply the needs of the people there is nothing being done which does not have some vital connection with the silk industry. No other district is so exclusively given up to the work as this one. (Howard and Buswell 1925, 15)

The intensiveness of sericulture in the Canton Delta was unparalleled in China. None of the other sericultural regions were capable of producing the number of harvests or generations per year of mulberry leaves and silkworms achieved by the four:six system in the Canton Delta. The sericultural area of the Lower Yangtze region, for instance, produced only two harvests of mulberry leaves and silkworms per year, regardless of land and labor investments.

In striking contrast, the tropical climate of the Canton Delta was ideal for the cultivation of a high-yielding variety of mulberry tree capable of supporting many generations of silkworms each year. The variety of mulberry cultivated, *Morus latifolia*, is the only mulberry capable of producing seven crops of leaves annually. The two varieties of silkworms raised, a bivoltine variety (Lun Uet) and a bivoltine-polyvoltine hybrid (Taai Cho), when forced to hatch by the watering method peculiar to the Delta, yielded six to nine—regularly seven—generations of silkworms annually (Howard and Buswell 1925, 68–69). Even excluding the special pre- and postseason generations of silkworms, seven generations meant that silkworms hatched almost monthly from March through October. The intensive labor associated with sericulture elsewhere was thus many times magnified in the four:six system of sericulture in the Canton Delta. According to the sericultural expert C. W. Howard, "In no place in the world is a silk producing region so organized and so concentrated as in South China" (1923, 32).

The Delta landscape was organized by the four:six system into a pattern that observers have described as visually stunning.

The "four-water-six-land" system may be carried out in various ways. Often the appearance at a distance is of a wide plain intersected by narrow canals. From a hill elevation in any one of the districts mentioned the sight is really wonderful. As far as the eye can reach in every direction there are fields of closely set dark green mulberry shrubs with the ponds of water scattered unequally between them and glistening in the sunshine. (Howard and Buswell 1925, 49)

The four:six system organized not only the landscape but also the pattern of settlement, which was described as unusual.

The silk towns in the province of Kwang-tung are very neat and clean, and, in many respects different from others through out the empire. Excepting those parts of the silk towns which are especially set apart for marketing, each house is detached and stands in its own mulberry plantation; partly, I suppose, because they are in consequence removed from noises and bad smells. The houses are generally large, and invariably built of bricks. The pathways which conduct the traveller from one silk town to another are well-paved. (Gray 1878, 2:228)

Sixty years later, geographer Glenn Trewartha was similarly struck by the unusual dispersed settlement pattern.

Nowhere else in Kwangtung Province do most of the farm houses stand alone and isolated outside of villages. Here the disseminated pattern of rural settlement predominates in the midst of what is otherwise a region of rural villages. The isolated farm houses of the silk region most commonly are of mud plaster mixed with straw which covers a wall made of mulberry skins woven into a wattle over cross pieces of bamboo. Grass thatch covers the high-gabled steep-sloping roofs. Village houses, especially those in larger settlements, more commonly have walls of brick and tile roofs. (Trewartha 1939, 9–10)

The dispersed pattern of settlement in the sericultural area would indeed have minimized "noises and bad smells," believed to affect the health of young silkworms adversely. Locating farmhouses in the midst of mulberry plantations also made economic sense because it minimized the labor and cost of transporting mulberry leaves to cocooneries. In addition, in an area where wealth was measured to a great extent in mulberry trees, farms located near mulberry groves may have been a means of safeguarding that wealth. Measures to protect mulberry wealth were apparently not always effective.

There are also bands who make a specialty robbing the mulberry trees. A company recently stole upon the Shun Tak [Sundak] community near Canton, with shears, ladders and bags. The villagers awoke to find their only wealth, the lusang trees, denuded of every branch and leaf. It is pretty hard to prove ownership of a mulberry leaf, but the worms of the adjoining Sai Kwan district proved to be exceedingly productive that season—so that the Shun Tak people retain their suspicions for a retaliatory raid next season. (Thomson 1909, 107)

Sericulture in the Canton Delta was big business. It has been estimated that 80 percent of the capital of Canton banks derived from Sundak sericulture (Howard and Buswell 1925, 16). Control of the sericultural industry did not lie with individual farmers. Although my own research focuses on the relationship of systems of sericulture and marriage at the level of individuals and their families, these families were linked in important ways to local gentry and lineage organizations. Much of the business of sericulture was organized by gentry and lineages, including the financing of farmers, maintenance of dikes, promotion of sericulture, and provision of market and transport protection services (see Eng 1986; So 1986; Hsieh, n.d.). Indeed, markets and steam-reeling factories, or filatures, were frequently owned by lineages: "Most of the filatures in Sui-tang are built by the clans. Each clan builds one or sometimes two filatures and rents them out, usually at the rate of ten per cent of the investment. The clans take great interest and pride in seeing that every girl or woman bearing their surname finds work, and is accumulating wealth. Many clans have become prosperous because of the filatures in their vicinity" (Lei and Lei 1925, 123).

In addition, most of the land itself was owned by lineages. It has been estimated that 35 percent of the cultivated land in all of Kwangtung province and an even higher proportion in the Canton Delta was lineage-owned (Chen 1936, ix). According to Chen Han-seng's estimates, the proportion of lineage-owned land to cultivated area was 40 percent in Naahmhoi, 50 percent in Punyu and Jungsaan, and 60 percent in Sundak (1936, 34). Howard and Buswell estimated that not more than 15 percent of the land in Sundak, Naahmhoi, and Jungsaan was owned by the farmers themselves; the remaining 85 percent was rented by farmers on leases of five to fifteen years (1925, 50).

THE DIVISION OF LABOR AND SILK TECHNOLOGY

Within the four:six system of sericulture in the delayed transfer marriage area, women participated in three main stages of the sericultural process: silkworm rearing, mulberry leaf harvesting, and silk reeling. Other stages, including mulberry cultivation and the marketing of eggs, leaves, and cocoons, were primarily men's work.

Informants described silkworm rearing as a family enterprise in which young and old participated (*gatihng gungjok*). With a new generation of silkworms hatching monthly for seven months, silkworm rearing was practically a year-round endeavor. Howard and Buswell report that on average a family with ten *mauh* of mulberry field could support silkworms hatched from two sheets of eggs, which usually yielded 140,000 to 160,000 cocoons (1925, 112). The life cycle of the silkworm from egg or "seed" to cocoon was traversed in approximately eighteen days of continuous hard work (Howard 1923, 21). During this time, the household was organized around the demands of the maturing silkworms, which required constant tending. In early growth periods, the worms required feeding every two hours, day and night. For each feeding, mulberry leaves had to be prepared and cut specifically for the age of the worms. In addition, worms had to be provided with proper light, temperature, and humidity and a clean environment, as well as to be protected from various noises, smells, and influences thought to affect their health and the condition of their silk adversely. For some tasks in silkworm rearing, worms had to be individually handled; for example, when they were ready to spin, they had to be placed on special spinning racks.

Informants reported that among women, wives were most involved in silkworm rearing. The division of labor for women in sericulture thus varied with marital status. As explained below, natolocally resident married women or bridedaughters characteristically reeled silk. Virilocally resident married women or wives assisted their husbands in raising silkworms.

The task of mulberry leaf harvesting was usually assumed by women, assisted by children, although in some places men harvested mulberry leaves, too. However, men were typically employed in performing the heavier aspects of worm rearing as well as in the transport and marketing of mulberry leaves. "When the first crop of leaves is ready, usually in April, thousands of boys, women, and girls are employed to strip them off, and pack them in baskets. Hundreds of men, in little boats propelled by paddles, dart back and forth along the canals, carrying these baskets of leaves to the market-places, where they are weighed by men detailed for that purpose" (Henry 1886, 66).

Almost forty years later, after the establishment of more than 160 steam filatures, an observer described a similar pattern of activity and division of labor. "During the silk worm season the mulberry fields are full of women and children each morning and evening picking leaves, and every road is processioned with men carrying baskets and every canal full of boats loaded with baskets of leaves going to the market in the morning and in the afternoon returning empty" (Howard 1923, 11).

Mulberry trees in the Delta were maintained as shrubs and not allowed to grow taller than four or five feet, a height easily managed by women harvesters. The actual harvesting was, as one informant explained, "not just a matter of picking leaves." Mulberry leaf harvesters had to know which leaves to pick and how to pick them in order to provide the silkworms with leaves of the right age and condition and to promote the growth of the next generation of leaves.

When the worms were ripe and ready to spin their cocoons, they were removed from the baskets in which they were raised and placed on bamboo spinning racks, called *bok*, peculiar to Delta sericulture (Howard and Buswell 1925, 91), usually by children. After the cocoons were spun, the chrysalises were killed by dry heat to prevent the silk moth from piercing the cocoon and damaging the silk. The spinning racks were stacked several layers thick in an inverted V-shape over a charcoal stove. A cloth was placed over the racks, leaving a vent hole at the top, and the cocoons were stifled in a slow heating process lasting several hours. This method of killing the chrysalis seemed fairly widespread among informants' villages and was apparently a long-established procedure.*

Following the stifling of the chrysalises, silk reeling was begun: "The silk cocoons, when ready to be unwound, are first plunged into hot water, and then set out to dry, after which the silk is unwound. Hundreds of women may be seen sitting by their doors winding the gossamer threads from the cocoons" (Henry 1886, 67).

The process of silk reeling or the unwinding of the silk fiber of the cocoon varied somewhat with the grade of cocoon. The basic procedure for reeling the best grade of cocoon entailed first soaking the cocoons in near-boiling water to soften the sericin, the gum binding the silk fibers. Softening loosened the outermost layers of silk, or floss, considered waste silk, which though unsuitable for reeling was used domestically as silk wadding in bedding and clothing. The removal of the floss, aided by the use

---

*In 1872, this same method had been reported as customary in the Canton area by an Austro-Hungarian expedition team reporting on sericulture (Scherzer 1872, *Anhang* 148).

of a brush and chopsticks, left exposed the middle layer of silk fiber that was reeled into silk thread. Cocoons were reeled directly from the basin of water. The silk fibers from several cocoons were picked up and reeled together, the number depending on the thickness of the thread desired. The fibers were passed through several guides or eyes and, before being wound onto the reel, were twisted to give the thread cohesion.

The earliest silk reels were hand-driven, the reel being either turned or cranked to wind up the silk. Improvements in silk reeling in the Canton Delta in the late nineteenth century were directed at the technology employed to power the reel and did not significantly change the basic unwinding procedure, that is, the manipulation of the cocoons in hot water. The history of reeling technology in the Canton Delta differed from that in the Lower Yangtze region. There, a foot-driven or treadle-reeling device had been widely employed since the seventeenth century. The traditional treadle-reeling machine was larger and heavier than a hand-reeling device and was best operated by men (Shih 1976, 11–12). Some versions of the traditional treadle required the labor of one operator, others two (Scherzer 1872, *Anhang* 148). The botanist Robert Fortune left this description of the traditional treadle employed in the Lower Yangtze region in the mid-nineteenth century: "Two men, or a man and a woman, are generally employed at each wheel. The business of one is to attend to the fire and to add fresh cocoons as the others are wound off. The most expert workman drives the machine with his foot and attends to the threads as they pass through the loops and over onto the wheel" (1857, 373).

Improved reeling technology, whether treadle or steam, transferred control of the reel from the hand, thereby freeing a second hand for manipulation of the silk thread. The use of two hands increased the reeler's control over the quality of thread produced. In addition, improved reeling technology increased the reeler's productivity. After the introduction of the traditional treadle in the Lower Yangtze, the hand reel continued to be employed because it was lighter and smaller and considered "more suitable for women." However, a reeler could produce only four taels of silk a day using a hand reel (1 tael was roughly 1.3 ounce) compared with twelve to thirteen taels and more on the traditional treadle-reeling device (Shih 1976, 12–13).

In striking contrast to the Lower Yangtze, the traditional treadle-reeling machine was apparently never employed in the Canton Delta. Before the mechanization of sericulture in the late nineteenth century, the hand reel seems to have been the only reeling technology known to the Delta (FSTC 1976, 4:28; Chung 1958, 260; Shih 1976, 83). Probably for this reason, the pre-mechanization reeling technology of the Delta has received little attention in the literature and is usually described only as simple or primitive. Since a number of features of Delta sericulture are distinctive to the area—including the four:six system, the egg-watering process (to force early hatching of silkworms), the cocoon-stifling procedure, and spinning racks—and are relevant to the development of marriage-resistance practices in the area, I have endeavored to secure as much detail as possible on the technology of reeling in the Delta before mechanization. The best source for this is a catalogue compiled by Isidore Hedde, a delegate of the French Ministry of Agriculture and Commerce who surveyed sericulture as practiced in several regions in China in 1843–46, twenty years before the introduction of the first steam-powered reeling machine.

Hedde described the device "employed by the people of Sundak" to reel silk and inventoried the different parts of the reeling apparatus, including the stove used to heat the water, the basin positioned over the stove from which the cocoons were reeled, the chopsticks used to manipulate the cocoons in the basin, the reeler's stool, and the clay containers for water, cocoons, and charcoal. "Then there is the silk reel over which the silk is wound and which the reeler turns with her left hand while using her right hand to manage the cocoons" (Hedde 1848, 139–40). The hand reel described by Hedde closely resembles the one still employed in the Delta during the post-mechanization era (Howard and Buswell 1925, 116). Finally, he observed of Sundak reeling technology, "The device is one of primitive simplicity and yet the crossing [the manner in which the silk fibers were twisted or crossed to produce a thread], called *la tavelle*, is one of the finest and most perfect that we found" (Hedde 1848, 140).*

The adoption of improved reeling technology in the Canton Delta in the late nineteenth century was in direct response to demands from American silk-weaving factories for an improved quality of raw silk, of uniform strength and thickness, that could be used on high-speed weaving machinery. In 1866, Ch'en Ch'i-yüan, an overseas merchant who had studied modern French reeling technology in Southeast Asia, introduced the steam-powered filature to the Canton Delta. He established the first filature in his native village, Gaan Chyun in the Sai Tiuh area of Naahmhoi (in the delayed transfer marriage area). By 1890, 75 percent of all raw silk exported through Canton was steam-reeled (calculated from China, Imperial Maritime Customs 1893, 554). Thus, the history of reeling technology in the Canton Delta differed markedly from that of the Lower Yangtze region. With the mechanization of silk reeling in the late nineteenth century, sericulture in the Canton Delta took a great technological leap from hand-driven reeling to steam-driven reeling, with profound consequences for the domestic sericultural industry.

The quality of the silk produced by the steam filatures was superior to hand-reeled silk and brought a higher price, about one-third more, on the export market (Shih 1976, 14). Because of the great demand for cocoons by steam filatures and their ability to pay a higher price, cocoons were diverted from the hand-reeling industry, and the local silk-weaving industry experienced a shortage of hand-reeled silk. There were eleven steam filatures in the Delta, employing 4,400 workers, by 1881 (Shih 1976, 14). During that same year, unemployment among local weavers caused by the steam filatures culminated in the famous

---

*This is an interesting observation since the later steam filatures reportedly used another crossing, the chambon system, which was inferior to the tavelle crossing that came to be used in the Shanghai filatures. See Eng 1986, 59–61.

1881 silk weavers' revolt in Naahmhoi; an organized band of weavers attacked and burned one filature and threatened another (Eng 1986, 48–49; So 1986, 111). The local magistrate took severe measures to quell the violence and prevent its spread, and Ch'en's own filature was closed and removed to Macau for three years. When he was invited to return and reopen his filature in 1884, Ch'en introduced a treadle-reeling machine, a transitional device developed to bridge the technological gap between steam reeling and hand reeling (FSTC 1976, 4:29). This treadle device improved the quality of silk that could be reeled in homes, thereby bolstering the lagging domestic silk-reeling industry and appeasing local silk weavers. This device, unlike the traditional treadle of the Lower Yangtze, was inexpensive and light, and it was quickly adopted in homes and treadle factories throughout the Delta.

Thus, two new reeling technologies—treadle reeling and steam reeling—were introduced in the Canton Delta in the late nineteenth century. Two distinct reeling industries developed, each occupying a different niche, differently organized and serving different markets. Although the hand-reeling technology was largely replaced by treadle technology in the domestic reeling industry, hand reeling remained viable in some areas (see below). The steam-reeling industry produced silk exclusively for export, supplying raw silk thread for the foreign weaving industry. During the peak period of filature production, roughly 1920–30, from 96 percent to 98 percent of the raw silk exported at Canton was reeled in steam filatures. In 1925, the year of greatest production, 53,482 piculs (around 3,600 tons) of steam-reeled silk were exported (Fong 1934, 491). During the same period, Howard and Buswell estimate that about twice as much silk was reeled on treadle reels as on steam-powered reels (1925, 118). Virtually all the treadle-reeled silk was sold on the domestic market. Thus, the post-mechanization era in the Canton Delta was characterized by three different reeling technologies, with different implications for bridedaughters and the practice of delayed transfer marriage.

THE LINK BETWEEN SERICULTURE AND
DELAYED TRANSFER MARRIAGE

In the Canton Delta, in both the pre- and post-mechanization eras, and in all three reeling technologies, silk reeling was the exclusive domain of women. Women were preferred as silk reelers. Informants explained that men did not reel silk because it was "fine" work (*hou saiji*) and "cultured" or "refined" work (*hou simahn*). As work performed exclusively by women, silk reeling can be contrasted with mulberry leaf harvesting, performed predominantly by women, and worm rearing, performed by men assisted by their wives. John Henry Gray provides an early description of silk reeling in the Delta:

Women and girls, carefully selected for the task, now unwind the cocoons—a process which they make easy by placing them in boiling water. These workers must be deft of hand and expert in the business, fully capable of making the threads of equal size, and of producing them bright, clear, and glossy. When the cocoons are put into boiling water, the outer layer, which is called the silk rind or shell, is first unwound. Another set of women and girls who are equally expert, are then engaged to unwind the inner layers of the cocoon, called the silk pulp or flesh. (Gray 1878, 2:223–24)

Certainly contributing to the cultural preference for women reelers were physical attributes, based in sexual dimorphism, that made women more effective reelers than men. The smaller and more delicate hands of women were better suited to manipulating the fine silk threads.

Women of all ages could reel silk, but age-related factors discriminated against younger girls and older women. Girls under the age of 10 did not reel. At 8 or 9, girls began a one- to two-year period of reeling instruction as apprentices to expert reelers, often older female relatives. The most skillful reelers were teenagers and young women, women favored with smooth and nimble hands and good eyesight. Smooth hands were the characteristic most often described by informants as influencing a woman's suitability for reeling. Since reeling was fine work, smooth hands, unroughened by age or years of labor, were important in handling the silk threads without breakage. Young women were also more nimble-fingered than older women, who were more likely to suffer from age-related diseases such as arthritis. Young women were also favored as reelers because good eyesight was a critical advantage in working with the fine silk threads for long hours during the post-harvest reeling periods. As discussed below, eyestrain resulting from filature reeling was a major constraint on reeling for older women.

Childlessness was another factor favoring the labor of young women. Silk reeling required constant visual attention and manual involvement over basins of near-boiling water for long hours. It was not a task that could be easily interrupted to tend to the demands of children.

When a cocoon is unwound a new thread must be thrown in. This is done with chop sticks and is a delicate process. If several cocoons become exhausted at once and new ones are not thrown in immediately then a thin spot results in the thread, which will break when the silk is put into the high power spinning machines in America. Constant watchfulness is necessary on the part of the women workers. If the water in the basins is not the right temperature winding is irregular and if fresh water is not put in frequently it becomes dirty and particles of dirt and broken bits of silk stick to the thread and cause defects.

· · · · ·

While the reeling woman is watching her threads and looking for cocoons to dropout she is holding in her left hand the ends of the threads of a lot of cocoons ready to be thrown in as needed. In water as hot as that of her reeling basin the gum on the cocoon threads is continually becoming softer and she must be constantly gathering around her finger the loosening ends of the fibres so as to keep them taut. (Howard 1923, 26, 133)

Of course, not all young women were childless. Childlessness as a criterion for reeling, therefore, generally discriminated between the marital statuses of bridedaughter and wife. Among young women, reeling favored the labor of bridedaughters, that is, childless married women, over wives. As shown below, the mechanization of silk reeling further increased the incompatibility between being a wife and being a silk reeler by requiring mobility. Wives with children and domestic responsibilities within their husband's home were less able to pursue employment in filatures.

One major effect of the mechanization of silk reeling was the specialization of reeling and its separation from the other stages in silk production, worm rearing and mulberry leaf harvesting. The specialization of reeling occurred primarily within the steam filature centers themselves, and it reinforced the association of silk reeling with bridedaughters. The features of filature reeling that reinforced this link included a longer reeling season, increased productivity, high wages, and mobility.

The length of the reeling season was primarily determined by the cocoon supply and the productivity of reelers. According to Gray, in the hand-reeling industry of the pre-mechanization era, "In the course of a day, one woman can unwind four taels of silk in weight. The most expert workers cannot, I believe, turn off more than five or six taels weight." As for the duration of post-harvest reeling, "Industrious workers who are masters require eighteen to nineteen days to finish one season or silk harvest; ordinary or second rate workers require twenty-four to twenty-five days to finish the same amount of work" (Gray 1878, 2:224).

On average, from the hatching of the eggs in one generation of silkworms to the hatching of eggs in the next required 34 days (Howard 1923, 21). Given the 18- to 25-day period needed to reel the cocoons from one harvest, we might expect that during the silk season (March–October) each cocoon harvest was followed by an intense period of reeling that ended before the next reeling period. Unfortunately, neither Gray nor other sources describe the organization of reeling at the domestic and village level during the pre-mechanization era. However, useful insights can be gained by considering the organization of reeling in the post-mechanization era outside filature centers, in areas specializing in mulberry and cocoon production and employing only treadle- and hand-reeling devices.

Informants from these areas frequently described a rotational pattern in which reelers within a village moved from one household to the next to help with reeling. Informants explained that a woman reeled first for her own family; she, of course, was not paid for this work. On finishing the family cocoon harvest, however, a reeler could work for a neighbor family that still had cocoons. For this labor she was compensated, although wages were usually less than half the best wage for filature reeling. Two cases, one from a village employing hand reels and the other from a village employing treadle reels, illustrate how reeling was organized at the domestic level.

A 74-year-old informant from Waih Hau, a multi-surname village outside Siu Laahm in Jungsaan, explained that the village produced mulberry leaves and silkworms primarily for export to silk-reeling centers. Mulberry leaves were sold in Siu Laahm on the mulberry markets, and silkworms were sold to filatures in Yuhng Keih and Gwai Jau in Sundak. Although girls in the village mostly worked harvesting mulberry leaves, they also reeled silk from cocoons saved for reeling in the homes. There were no treadle-reeling machines in the village, and women reeled at home by hand. If a family needed more reelers, they hired neighbor girls. When the family harvest was done, girls went to reel for other families.

A 59-year-old informant from a single-surname village in Gong Meih in Sundak recalled that there were no steam filatures in Gong Meih and that villagers cultivated mulberry and raised worms mainly for export to reeling centers. Village girls harvested mulberry leaves, cut grass, and reeled silk at home. The informant remembered seeing older female relatives, including her elder sister, reel silk by hand. Neighbor women worked together to reel the cocoons after the harvests. Later, the villagers used treadle-driven reels. The informant herself had reeled on such a machine. She explained that although the treadle machines, like hand-reeling devices, were still used in homes, families had to hire women from neighboring villages to help with the reeling. In her village, each family usually hired four to five people from neighboring villages to help with reeling immediately after the harvests.

Treadle machines were employed not only in homes but in treadle factories, some of which had as many as 200 to 300 treadle-reeling machines. On a more intermediate scale, there were also what might be called treadle workshops. Other informants from these areas peripheral to filature centers described reeling in ancestral halls, where families took turns reeling.

Characterizing all silk reeling beyond filature centers was the participation of reelers in other stages of the sericultural process, especially mulberry leaf harvesting. After completing the reeling of one harvest of cocoons, reelers became mulberry leaf harvesters. This pattern of alternating reeling and harvesting emerged in all descriptions of reeling in areas employing only hand and treadle devices during the post-mechanization era. In all probability, the reeling season in the pre-mechanization era was also characterized by slack periods after the reeling for one harvest of cocoons was completed when reelers worked as mulberry leaf harvesters.

By contrast, in post-mechanization filature centers, silk reeling was a highly specialized task, and informants reported that women who reeled silk refused to pick mulberry leaves for fear of spoiling their hands for reeling. In addition, informants' accounts indicate that filature reelers considered mulberry leaf harvesting an inferior task.

A 72-year-old informant from Gaan Chyun in the Sai Tiuh area of Naahmhoi, the site of the very first steam filature, said that many women in the Sai Tiuh area had reeled silk in local filatures, as she had herself. She explained that if a woman reeled silk, she did not harvest mulberry leaves because a reeler needed skillful, smooth hands. Not only would she not work as a mulberry leaf harvester, a reeler also did no housework that roughened her hands. According to the informant, a reeler with rough hands was unable to do fine work. In addition, mulberry leaf harvesting was lower-status work than silk reeling. Of course, if a reeler's father raised mulberry, then she helped him with the harvest. Most filature reelers, however, did not work harvesting mulberry leaves. That was a job for older women.

Some reelers even hired muijai to serve them and perform household chores.

Reelers in filatures could specialize in reeling because such work approached full-time employment. Steam filatures could not afford to operate part-time or at partial capacity. They could not afford to hire and fire with each harvest, explained one informant. Filatures had to maintain production for the duration of the silk season. Therefore, they purchased large lots of cocoons, which they warehoused, and reelers worked twelve hours a day, seven days a week, sometimes for ten months and longer. A 90-year-old informant boasted that most girls in the reeling center of Yuhng Keih in Sundak reeled silk in steam filatures where they could work for nearly the whole year, except for a short break of less than a month at the New Year. A study of filatures in one reeling center, Seui Tuhng in Sundak, showed that the long hours and the long season—as well as the hot and steamy filature environment with temperatures of 90° F and above—took its toll on reeler attendance, which was reported as irregular (Lei and Lei 1925, 149). Bonuses were offered as incentives for perfect attendance.

In addition to lengthening the reeling season, filature employment also intensified the reeling experience by increasing productivity. The shift from hand to treadle to steam reeling brought progressively higher levels of reeler productivity. During the pre-mechanization era, as noted earlier, hand reelers usually produced four taels of raw silk per day, although "expert workers" produced as much as five to six taels. During the post-mechanization era, treadle reelers produced eight taels of raw silk per day (Howard and Buswell 1925, 120). In steam filatures, according to informants, reelers were set a quota of ten taels per day; they were fined for producing only eight taels and rewarded with bonuses for producing as many as twelve.*

For the individual reeler, steam filature employment meant a two- or threefold increase in productivity over hand reeling, but this in turn increased demands on reelers' eyes. In fact, sources cite eyestrain as a major constraint on long-term employment in filatures. "The reeling room is usually too dark for such delicate work and the eyes of the reelers are very much taxed to see the fine silk thread which they are reeling. Older women are seldom seen at the basins for the reason their eyes have succumbed to the strain put on them earlier" (Howard and Buswell 1925, 122). As they are unwound from the silk cocoons, the fine silk fibers can only be described as resembling spiderweb. In a tour of a silk factory in Yuhng Keih in 1986, I watched silk reelers deftly thread the fine silk filaments—which I could scarcely see—through the slight eyes of the reeling apparatus. Each reeler simultaneously managed twenty different threads, each made up of the fibers of sixteen different cocoons. It was apparent that even in a modern silk-reeling factory, eyestrain would still be a major constraint on long-term employment. The factory supervisor observed that the younger women with their better eyesight were more skillful reelers, but that the older women continued to reel through "feel," relying less on their eyes and more on their experience.

The significance of age as a constraint on reeling increased with mechanization, and yet the age of employees varied somewhat. Howard and Buswell report that filature reelers ranged in age from 13 to 25, with most reelers aged 20 to 25 (1925, 140). However, Lei Yue-wai and Lei Hei-kit, also of Ling Nan Agricultural College, who studied the steam filatures (and in particular one filature) in Seui Tuhng in Sundak, reported: "The ages of

---

*Some versions of the treadle-reeling apparatus were more advanced than others, as I saw during a tour of the silk country in 1986. According to a local silk expert, a reeler using the simplest and perhaps earliest version of the treadle device could manage fewer cocoons than with a more advanced treadle device. It would also seem that productivity varied with the version of treadle device used. Howard and Buswell's figure of eight taels of raw silk for treadle reelers in 1925 may well be for those who used the most advanced treadle devices of the day.

the women range from 13 to 45 years, 20 to 30 being the most common. A woman will get her best wage when she is 25 to 30 years of age, if she was trained when young" (1925, 133).

This variation in the age of filature reelers can probably be explained by variation in the quality of the filatures and of the reelers themselves. Lei and Lei describe three classes of filatures in the Delta, differentiated on the basis of the quality of silk produced, as reflected in price. First-class filatures produced a superior grade of silk with the aid of improvements in physical plant and the selection of first-rate reelers. The filatures in Seui Tuhng studied by Lei and Lei were third-class filatures, the most common class, and employed reelers from 13 to 45 years old who were paid half the wage paid to reelers in first-class filatures (1925, 133, 150).* Even in third-class filatures producing the lowest grade of silk, however, age was a primary consideration in the reckoning of a reeler's wage.

To judge a woman's work, upon which her wage is determined, the foreman takes into consideration many factors. Firstly, the age of the woman. Secondly, the temperament and disposition, which they can judge by her behavior and the appearance of her face. Thirdly, cleanliness and orderliness of work. Fourthly, the quantity of cocoons a woman puts into the basin at one time. This becomes a habit and the women are slow to change when told to put in less. Fifthly, the amount of pulling and motion which the reeling girl exerts with her left hand on the ends of the cocoon fibers. The less pulling the better. Sixthly, the quantity and quality of silk a girl can finish from a given quantity of cocoons in a day. (Lei and Lei 1925, 134)

The situation apparently differed in first-class filatures. Although good comparative data are unavailable, Lei and Lei report that in filatures in Yuhng Keih producing the most expensive grade of silk and paying top wages, reelers were "more skillful" (1925, 150). Reelers in first-class filatures had to conform to higher standards of performance and were assessed heavy fines for work that fell short of these standards. Age, an

---

*In a present-day silk filature in Yuhng Keih in Sundak, the age of silk reelers ranges from 16 to 50, according to the supervisor. The most skillful reelers are in their twenties and thirties.

important criterion for reeling even in third-class filatures, was surely a more significant criterion in employment in first-class filatures. Howard and Buswell's report of a 13–25 age range in filatures may well reflect the age composition in first-class filatures. High wages for filature employment further reinforced the link between silk reeling and bridedaughters. The prime motivation for seeking work as a silk reeler for both daughters and their parents was the high wages offered in Delta filatures, which were higher than those in the Lower Yangtze region (Li Kolu 1927, 49). Informants boasted of their ability as silk reelers to earn high wages.

A 74-year-old informant from the urban part of Daaih Leuhng in Sundak, a filature reeling center, reported that most girls and bridedaughters reeled silk, whereas wives harvested mulberry leaves and helped their husband's family with silkworm rearing. Silk reelers earned a lot of money in Daaih Leuhng, much more than in jobs like mulberry leaf harvesting. Reelers could earn more than a dollar a day. Therefore, a silk reeler's contribution to her family was the most important, because she could earn the most, even more than her brothers. A male laborer couldn't earn as much as a silk reeler, she explained, because his wages were not constant but depended on harvests. Because silk reelers in Daaih Leuhng earned such a lot of money, they didn't have to depend on others. That's why, even when they married, silk reelers didn't like being married to men who earned less than they did.

The introduction of treadle technology may have also substantially increased the disposable income of bridedaughters. The amount of disposable income was determined both by wage levels and by the period of employment outside the natal home. Although I do not have data on wage levels for hand reeling in the pre-mechanization era, the opportunity for reeling outside the family must have been limited to post-harvest reeling periods. With the establishment of treadle-reeling workshops and factories and the consequent extension of the reeling season, bridedaughters in areas peripheral to filature centers enjoyed an increased opportunity to reel outside the home and, therefore, possibly a considerable increase in income.

The ability of reelers to make substantial contributions to natal families in the post-mechanization era increased their prestige within those families and enhanced their self-esteem. This heightened self-esteem was reflected in comments by informants from filature centers that "girls were better than boys because they could contribute more to their family" and "girls were smarter than boys because they could reel silk." The self-esteem of the filature reelers was apparent even to onlookers.

Only as we neared big market towns, in which silk filatures belched forth the stench of cocoons, did we come upon better homes and fewer careworn faces. The daughters of such families were spinners. It was then that I began to see what industrialism, bad as it had seemed elsewhere, meant to the working girls. These were the only places in the whole country where the birth of a baby girl was an occasion for joy, for here girls were the main support of families. Consciousness of their worth was reflected in their dignified independent bearing. (Smedley 1943, 89)

In spite of working conditions the women in the filatures seem to be alert and active and happy. The wages they receive are higher than they can get in any other place and they are eager for the work. The reeling women can be recognized in a filature town because they are always dressed better and show a better physical appearance. (Howard and Buswell 1925, 143)*

By enhancing the prestige and independence of reelers, high wages contributed to the anti-marital bias among bridedaughters. Informants described silk reelers as typically anxious to avoid pregnancy and to postpone settling with their husband. As one Sundak informant explained, "Sometimes silk reelers

---

*A silk reeler's ability to earn the highest wage depended, as discussed above, on factors such as the location and class of the filature in which she worked and on her age and skill. Even for reelers earning the highest wage, however, working conditions were poor. In 1912 and 1925, silk reelers in Sundak struck for better working conditions and higher pay. See Eng (1986, 65–66).

wanted to work longer than the usual four- to six-year separation, and they delayed returning to their husband." Their parents, too, were anxious to extend the intervals of postmarital separation and to delay the departure of bridedaughters whose filature wages were a major contribution to family income. In parental perceptions, therefore, continued benefits from filature reeling were linked to the extension of postmarital separations, that is, of the bridedaughter stage in a woman's life cycle.

Another feature of filature employment, the increased mobility of filature reelers, also reinforced the link between bridedaughters and reeling. As early as the establishment of the first filature in 1866, the mobility of the reeling labor force was a concern for filature owners and parents of reelers. In Ch'en's original filature, which had 300 reeling basins, 130 reelers were recruited from Gaan Chyun itself, and the rest were from nearby villages (So 1986, 108). Even in the era of peak employment in the 1920's, the older generation remained anxious about the mobility required of their daughters:

A 70-year-old informant from a village near Siu Laahm in Jungsaan, an area beyond the filature centers and one specializing in only the mulberry-cultivation and worm-rearing stages of sericulture, said that most girls in her village worked as mulberry leaf harvesters. Girls also did silk reeling, not in filatures but in homes, where they made only small wages. She explained that few girls from her village went to reel in filatures in Yuhng Keih and Gwai Jau, where a reeler could earn much more, because the older generation would not allow daughters to travel to distant villages.

Even though filatures were hardly concentrated (they were found in at least 56 places)* they were not evenly distributed across the landscape. The drawing power of high wages for filature employment was considerable, both for reelers themselves, who retained a portion of their wages, and for their families. For

*Based on tallies provided by Howard and Buswell 1925, 15–32.

parents, however, the benefits of high wages had to be weighed against the risks of mobility, that is, against the loss of control over daughters in distant filature centers. Mobility fostered a spirit of independence among silk reelers that contributed to their anti-marital bias. For this reason, parents were especially reluctant to allow young unmarried daughters to migrate to filature centers.

For many reelers in my informants' generation, filature employment meant a daily commute to a neighboring village. For others, filature employment meant leaving natal villages and taking up residence in one of the dormitories built by the filatures to accommodate workers. According to a 72-year-old Sundak informant, filatures in Yuhng Keih established dormitories for reelers from distant villages, and rang bells to let reelers in nearby villages know when to get up in the morning, when to leave for the filatures, and when to be at their basins in the filatures.

The demand for a mobile labor force favored the labor of bridedaughters, who as older, natolocally resident daughters encountered fewer restrictions on their mobility and were already (or so their parents hoped) committed to marriage. For wives, the need for mobility only increased the incompatibility between employment in filature reeling and their domestic responsibilities in their husband's home. Thus, in addition to the increased length of the reeling season, higher reeler productivity, and high earnings for filature employment, the need for mobility reinforced the link between reeling and bridedaughters.

THE RISE OF MARRIAGE-RESISTANCE PRACTICES

In reinforcing both the link between silk reeling and bridedaughters and the anti-marital bias among women, filature employment was the prime factor in the efflorescence of compensation marriage, the earliest of the popular alternatives to customary delayed transfer marriage. The growth of filature employment in the Canton Delta can be seen in the rise in the num-

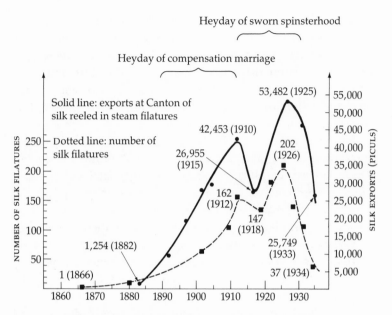

Fig. 1. Marriage alternatives and the growth of the steam filature industry. Sources: China, Imperial Maritime Customs, 1893, 554, and 1906,
2:177; Fong 1934, 491; Chung 1958, 262.

ber of filatures and in the amount of steam-reeled silk produced,
both of which are indicators of the growing impact of high
wages and mobility on bridedaughters. Figure 1 plots the hey-
days of compensation marriage and sworn spinsterhood against
the number of filatures and amount of steam-reeled silk produced. The rise of compensation marriage clearly parallels the
rise in filature employment, the early source of compensation
funds. Filature reeling as the economic basis for compensation
marriages is also supported by informants' accounts. As noted
earlier, many informants spoke of filature reelers and compensating bridedaughters as synonymous (see Chapter 3).

Estimates of the number of silk reelers employed in filatures
are based on the number of filatures and basins or reeling machines per filature. Sources frequently disagree over the number
of filatures. These discrepancies can be attributed to the high
failure rate among filatures, the fact that not all filatures oper-

ated every year, and the time of year when filature surveys were conducted (Lillian Li 1981, 240 n5; Eng 1978, 62).* Howard and Buswell reported that the number of basins per filature ranged from 100 basins for the smallest filature on record to 760 basins for the largest. As a result of their survey in 1923–25, they found that roughly half of the filatures had between 400 and 500 basins, one-fourth had 500 to 700 basins, and one-fourth had 200 to 400 basins (1925, 122). Their figure of 167 filatures in 1925 gives a rough estimate of from 63,000 to 87,000 filature reelers. Other estimates are 136,860 reelers for 1928,[†] and more than 100,000 for 1922 (FSTC 1976, 4:31).

Of course, these estimates suggest only the number of reelers at a given point in time whose lives and families were affected by their employment in filatures. The 1920's followed more than fifty years of development in the filature reeling industry and of employment of bridedaughters in that industry. In addition, since filatures were not evenly distributed over the sericultural area, the direct impact of filature employment—the effect of specialization, high wages, and mobility—was greater in some areas than in others. In the Howard and Buswell survey, 135 of the 167 documented filatures were located in one county, Sundak (1925, 18). More than half those filatures were located in one district within Sundak, District V (FSTC 1976, 4:31).

Map 4 plots the distribution of compensation marriage against sericultural technology in the Delta for the 1920's. The number of filatures in Sundak is shown by district, which roughly corresponded to delta tracts (or parts of tracts). The triangle filature symbol precedes the number of filatures in each district. Thus, District V boasted 78 filatures, whereas Districts VIII and IX had none. Of the filatures located outside Sundak, most—35—were located in the general vicinity of Sai Tiuh Gun

---

*The discrepancies may also result from different systems of reckoning. In the twentieth century, many treadle-reeling workshops and small factories used steam to heat the water for the reeling basins, and may therefore have been counted among the modern steam filatures (FSTC 1976, 4:29).

†From a Japanese survey published in Ide Kiwata, 1939, *Shina no sangyō to keizai* (The industries and economy of South China) (Tokyo); cited in Eng 1978, 63.

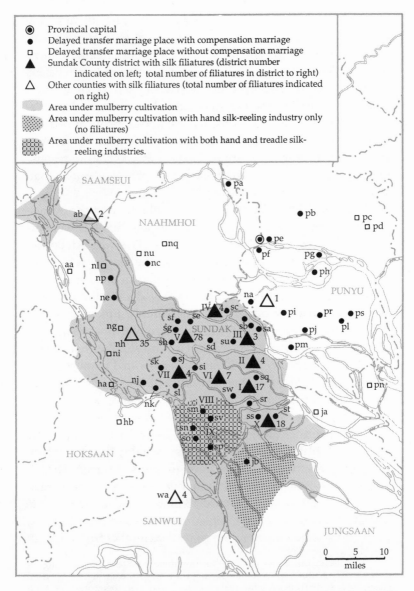

SAAMSEUI

● pa

ab △ 2
        NAAHMHOI
                                    ● pb   □ pc
                                                □ pd
                            □ nq   ◉ ● pe
                    □ nu   pf   pg ●
aa   ● nc
□   nl □   ● ph
    np ●
                                    na   PUNYU
● ne   △ 1
                                                ● pi   ● pr   ● ps
        ng □   sf   IV ▲ 4 ● sc   pl
            △ 35 sg ● SUNDAK sb ● sa   ● pj
nh   V ▲ 78   III ▲ 3   ● pm
□ ni   sh   sd su ●
            sk ● sj   si   II ▲ 4
ha □   nj   VII ▲ 4 VI ▲ 7   ● sq   □ pn
            ● sl   sw I ▲ 17
        nk   VIII   sr   st
            sm   sv   ss   X ▲ 18   □ ja
            sn   IX   sp ●
            so ●
HOKSAAN   ● jb

            wa △ 4

        SANWUI   JUNGSAAN

                                    0   5   10
                                    miles

Map 4: The distribution of compensation marriage and sericultural
technology in the 1920's. See Appendix C for place-name identification.

Saan (nh) in Naahmhoi. Two filatures were located in Saamseui at Sai Naahm (ab), and four in Sanwui near Gong Muhn (wa). There was only one filature in Punyu, at Sehk Bihk near Lahm Ngohk (na) in Naahmhoi. There were no filatures in Hoksaan and Jungsaan (Howard and Buswell 1925, 15–25; FSTC 1976, 4:30–33). Informants reported that in the filature areas, treadle-reeling machines were used at home and in treadle workshops and factories to reel the "extra" or inferior cocoons not sold to filatures. No hand reeling was reported in the filature area. In Districts VIII and IX in Sundak, where there were no filatures, informants reported the use of both treadle- and hand-reeling machines. In the Siu Laahm area (jb) of Jungsaan, where there were no filatures and mulberry was raised for export to Sundak, informants reported that reeling was done on hand-reeling devices only and that treadle-reeling machines were not used. In the part of Naahmhoi bordering Saamseui (nl), characterized by a mixed economy based on sericulture and farming, mulberry was reportedly raised strictly for export to filature centers, and no reeling was done in the villages.

As shown on Map 4, by the 1920's compensation marriage also occurred beyond the filature centers. This can probably be attributed both to the seasonal migration of female laborers into the sericultural area and to the late expansion of the economic base of compensation marriage with the rise of domestic service. However, the tradition of compensation marriage ran deepest in the filature centers. There, informants report both a greater incidence of compensation marriage among relatives, friends, and fellow-villagers and a greater tolerance of that marriage alternative. In addition, compensation marriage was most elaborated in filature centers, occurring there in two forms (the late form, in which bridedaughters compensated after several years of marriage, and the early or immediate form, in which bridedaughters compensated before marriage and were married on the same day as the secondary wife). In sericultural areas where there was no filature reeling, such as Gong Meih in Sundak and Siu Laahm in Jungsaan, the early form of compensation was not reported.

The spatial referent of the sequence of changes in marriage resistance that I have posited—compensation marriage, bride-initiated spirit marriage, sworn spinsterhood—is the filature centers of Sundak. The full spectrum of marriage alternatives occurred there, including the early form of compensation marriage and bride-initiated spirit marriage, which was practiced almost exclusively in Sundak. The sequence of changes was abbreviated in the outlying areas, where often only the late form of compensation marriage and sworn spinsterhood were practiced. In a few cases, only sworn spinsterhood was practiced. Sworn spinsterhood enjoyed a wider distribution than compensation marriage, in part because of the greater range of economic opportunities for women in that later era and in part because it was a less expensive marriage option. Thus, in the case of the villages in Naahmhoi near Saamseui (nl), where there were no filatures and no reeling, both informants reported that they had never heard of the practice of compensation marriage in that area, but that a few women had practiced sworn spinsterhood. Since most sworn spinsters (and compensating bridedaughters) from outlying areas migrated to filature and service centers, it would be difficult to establish a separate chronology of marriage alternatives for the outlying areas. My own sense is that sworn spinsterhood occurred later in those areas peripheral to filature centers and that its popularity spread from Sundak.

A FINAL NOTE ON THE SILK INDUSTRY

Although an analysis of the contemporary sericultural industry in the Canton Delta is beyond the scope of the present study, a few observations may help to set this study in historical perspective. The blows dealt the local silk industry in the 1920's and 1930's, including the collapse of the international market for silk with the world depression, initiated a period of decline from which the industry never recovered. Since the establishment of the People's Republic, new economic priorities have prevailed. On a tour of the silk country in 1986, arranged by the Sundak

County Association of Hong Kong, my research assistant and I were surprised to see so little mulberry growing in the heart of what was once the great silk-producing district. The local official who was our guide observed that most land once devoted to mulberry plantations has been converted to sugarcane, a more lucrative enterprise. In Daaih Leuhng, a former silk center in Sundak, our guide tried to find an example of the traditional diked mulberry grove fish pond mode of sericulture—complete with cocoonery and spinning racks—but she was able to locate only one, and the worms were too young to show. We therefore set out for villages in Gong Meih, also in Sundak county, that were more rural in character. Finding our example of diked mulberry grove fish pond sericulture at last in the village of Seuhng Chyun in Gong Meih, we spoke with our guide, another local official, and the village head about the prospects for sericulture in the future. The village head, who, like his father and grandfather before him, raises mulberry, predicted that within a few years there would be no mulberry cultivated even in Seuhng Chyun.

There were other surprises on this tour. At two different cocoon stations, where cocoons are sorted and baled before being sent to the modern silk filatures, we were shown two different treadle-reeling machines still in use. (It was only because our local guides knew that I was interested in the history of silk-reeling technology in the Canton Delta that we were shown machines that everyone present acknowledged to be old-fashioned.) The old treadle-reeling machines are now used at cocoon stations to establish the quality of the cocoons, whose price depends on how much silk a measure of cocoons will produce. At the larger cocoon station, about a dozen treadle-reeling machines, constructed of metal and wood, formed a single unit, as in a workshop. The reeling basins were set in a row in a long counter, under which ran a pipe to heat the water. Behind the counter were the reelers' stools, and behind each stool was a silk reel, which the reeler operated by depressing a treadle board. On the day of our visit, four young women were busy reeling silk to test cocoons. A bigger surprise awaited us at the smaller of the two cocoon stations. There on the earthen floor stood a treadle-reeling apparatus, utterly simple in design and constructed of wood, apparently a much earlier version of the treadle technology in operation at the larger cocoon station. This treadle-reeling apparatus required a small traditional stove, which was set on the ground and on which the pot containing the reeling water was heated. In every detail, this apparatus fit the description informants had given us of the treadle-reeling device "with a big wheel" that was used in homes in the 1920's and earlier.

Conclusion

The variation in marriage practices in the Canton Delta, long noted as unique in Chinese society, cannot be explained apart from the underlying social system. That social system was characterized not by major marriage but by delayed transfer marriage, the norm throughout an extensive area of the Delta in both sericultural and agricultural villages. Although we do not yet know the economic conditions under which delayed transfer marriage originated in Chinese society in the Canton Delta, it seems clear that that marriage system persisted best—and even flourished—in sericulture. Delayed transfer marriage could not have originated in response to labor demands within the sericultural industry, but in due course it became functionally linked to sericulture through the association of silk reeling with the status of bridedaughter. The economic value of bridedaughters in sericultural areas led to longer periods of postmarital separation, as natal families and lineages sought to retain their married daughters for the valuable labor they performed. Even in the

pre-mechanization era, bridedaughters must have enjoyed enhanced prestige within their natal homes as a result of their labor contributions. In addition, longer periods of natolocal residence must have reinforced the bridedaughter's identity with
her natal family and her reluctance to settle permanently in her
husband's home. Both enhanced prestige and longer periods of
separation contributed to the growth of an anti-marital bias
among young women in the sericultural area, an important social precondition for the rise of marriage-resistance practices in
the wake of the mechanization of silk reeling.

The mechanization of reeling strengthened the position of
bridedaughters as preferred reelers and increased the market
value of their labor. Filature employment thus provided the economic basis for a still more radical extension of the customary
period of postmarital separation, achieved through the payment
of compensation to the husband's family. I have shown how the
rise of compensation marriage as an alternative to customary delayed transfer marriage paralleled the growth of employment in
the steam-reeling industry. In addition, I have shown that it was
not modern economic change per se that caused the rise of compensation marriage, but rather the impact of economic change
on the distinctive delayed transfer form of marriage. Compensation marriage took its shape from the underlying delayed transfer marriage system and can be understood only in the context
of that marriage system.

In addition, it appears that compensation marriage was in
effect a specialized form of compensation as a general means of
renegotiating marriage contracts. Bridedaughters of the late
nineteenth century adopted compensation as a means to achieve
independence from husbands and affines. Compensation marriage was the first of several marriage-resistance practices that
evolved to meet the needs of young women and their families at
the turn of the century. A certain developmental logic is apparent in the sequence of the several alternatives to delayed transfer
marriage. Compensation marriage was expensive for young
women, who found in sworn spinsterhood greater freedom—

from marriage altogether—at less cost. There was no lump-sum payment equivalent to compensation required of women who became spinsters, a fact not lost on the women themselves. If sworn spinsterhood was cheaper, it was also simpler. Unlike compensation marriage, spinsterhood was not disruptive of relations between families or lineages. However, although sworn spinsterhood seems a logical successor to compensation marriage, overcoming many of the difficulties inherent in that early marriage-resistance practice, it was also a more radical proposition. Nonmarriage raised new and different problems: What was to be done with an unmarried daughter at death and with her tablet afterward? These were troubling matters for both the spinster and her natal family. An early solution was found in the practice of bride-initiated spirit marriage. Marriage to a deceased man provided a spinster with the benefits of marriage—a host for spirit and tablet—without the primary disadvantage of marriage, the claims and obligations presented by a living husband and his parents. Another, later solution, preferable to spirit marriage, was the spinster house. Spinster houses provided not only a host for spirit and tablet after death, but also a suitable residence in life.

Sworn spinsterhood offered silk reelers the ultimate mobility to pursue filature employment. But by the 1930's, with the world depression, the growing significance of the synthetic fiber industry, the Japanese occupation, and civil war, sericulture—the economic basis for sworn spinsterhood—collapsed. Increasingly, spinsters turned to domestic service in Hong Kong, Singapore, and Macau to support themselves and their families. This shift in the economic base for spinsterhood was noted in the publication "The Contribution of Kwangtung Women to the Worm and Silk Industry" (Liao 1934). According to this report, after 1929 more than 100,000 women formerly engaged in some phase of the silk industry were without work. These unemployed silk workers for the most part turned to Canton and other cities seeking work as domestic servants.

To students of China, the delayed transfer marriage system

itself is perhaps more exciting than the marriage-resistance practices that arose within it. As described in Chapter 1, delayed transfer marriage was unknown to me when I undertook my original research in 1979. Over the following two-and-a-half years—as the contours of the delayed transfer marriage system became apparent—it seemed increasingly clear to me that the origins of that system lay in some early fusion of local non-Chinese or "non-Han" cultures with Han Chinese culture. This cultural fusion produced the distinctive version of Chinese society found in the Canton Delta.*

The delayed transfer area and greater Canton Delta are situated in the Lingnan region, a physiographic macroregion defined by the drainage basin that includes the West, North, and East rivers (Skinner 1977). A cursory search of the literature on non-Han groups in the Lingnan region yields several examples of a delayed transfer type of marriage. Delayed transfer has been documented in Kweichow province among the P'u-i people at Tu-shan in the Lingnan region (Chao and Chün 1981), and more generally among the P'u-i in Kweichow (Kung and Shih 1981; Mo 1981).[†] In Kwangsi, a delayed transfer type of marriage has been reported among an unidentified people at I-shan (Hu 1935, 25–26). Most significantly, delayed transfer marriage has been established among the Chuang, the largest non-Han ethnic group in Kwangsi province as well as in all of China (Eberhard, cited in Wiens 1967, 53). In addition, on Hainan island, delayed transfer marriage has been documented among the Li peoples. The German anthropologist Hans Stübel, who conducted fieldwork among the Li in the 1930's, made the significant observation that the length of the interval of separation for husbands and wives in the different Li groups varied with degree of sinicization. In the least sinicized groups, separation until the birth of the first child was practiced, whereas among groups more

---

*This conclusion is also suggested by Shirokogoroff (1931), Eberhard (1968, 135–36), and Lin (1981, 285).

[†]Mo 1981 and Kung and Shih 1981 report that delayed transfer among the P'u-i in Kweichow province is known as the custom of "not sitting" in the husband's family (pu tso-chia).

heavily influenced by Chinese culture, husbands and wives were separated for only the first three days of marriage (1976, 83:76–77).

It may well prove significant that all three Lingnan ethnic groups identified as practicing delayed transfer marriage—P'u-i, Chuang, Li—are Tai-speaking groups, members of the Tai-Kadai language stock (Benedict 1942; Lebar et al. 1964; Pulleyblank 1983). The history of the settlement of the Lingnan region was one of intimate interaction between Sinitic and Tai peoples. The long process of "sinification" may well be more a complex tale of mutual cultural influence and cultural fusion than was earlier thought (Lebar et al. 1964; Pulleyblank 1983; Moser 1985). This is certainly suggested by my own work. A definitive account is, of course, beyond the scope of the present work and must await the outcome of future research.

From my own research in the delayed transfer marriage area of the Canton Delta, I am able to identify four features that may be the legacy or vestiges of an older "cultural complex": delayed transfer marriage, girls' houses, boys' houses, and the practice of marriage at night. Both delayed transfer marriage and girls' houses have received detailed consideration in this book. Boys' houses and marriage at night are a fainter legacy, but a perceptible one nonetheless. As noted earlier, boys' houses also occurred in at least parts of the area in which girls' houses were traditional, but their distribution is less certain.* The anthropologists Robert F. Spencer and S. A. Barrett discuss "bachelor houses" in a village in Jungsaan county (1948). My own informants from villages in the delayed transfer marriage area only very occasionally reported boys' houses. Unfortunately, with so little information, we can conclude only that by the early twentieth century boys' houses were not common in the delayed transfer marriage area. As one informant commented, "Boys didn't need boys' houses because they had ancestral halls!"

* According to Stübel, "youth houses" where boys and girls grouped together were found on Hainan among the Li peoples (1976, 83:75, 225). Eberhard finds the distribution of boys' or men's houses in South China to correspond to the area under the influence of Tai culture (1942, 325).

The fourth feature of the posited older cultural complex is the practice of marriage at night. Although a few of my informants described this practice, my inquiries did not elicit consistent responses. In the Republican era, the practice of marriage at night was documented by K'ai Shih for the Delta county of Goumihng. There, it was targeted for "reform"—along with delayed transfer marriage itself—by the Goumihng Custom Reform Association. Families were instructed to advise their daughters to enter the bridal sedan chair "while the sun is still up" (K'ai 1926, 940). In the orthodox view, marriage at night implied that a family had something to hide. In the mid-nineteenth century, John Henry Gray described marriage at night as customary in some districts surrounding Canton (1878, 1:187). This practice is also mentioned in the Customs section of the 1871 edition of the gazetteer for Punyu county. In a more tenuous reference, Alvaro (Alvarez) Semmedo, a Portuguese Jesuit father who lived at the Chinese court and in "other cities" for 22 years, describes marriage at night as customary in some of the southern provinces: "In other Provinces, especially towards the South, the Bride-groome sendeth the sedan toward the evening . . . and a great deal of company . . . waite upon her with lights set in wooden frams like lanthornes" (1655, 72).

A comparison of delayed transfer marriage as practiced in traditional Chinese society in Kwangtung and Fukien may in the future shed further light on the origin of that marriage system. Since the practice of delayed transfer marriage varied even within the Canton Delta, however, we should expect that a comparison of its practice in different regions will reflect different developmental histories, and perhaps a different fusion of cultures. Lin Hui-hsiang's 1951 report on delayed transfer marriage in Hui-an county in Fukien suggests several points of departure, although the basic structure of delayed transfer marriage seems the same: Brides separated from their husband on the third day of marriage, resuming residence in their natal home for at least the first two or three years of marriage, visiting the husband's family on festival occasions, and returning to settle in the husband's home on first pregnancy (1981, 255).* Significantly, Lin makes no mention of girls' houses. This is probably not a simple oversight or a matter of focus, for Lin provides evidence of the close bonds between local women, describing the effectiveness of social sanctions meted out by "sisters" who monitored the marital conduct of bridedaughters (1981, 256). Furthermore, Lin is quick to describe an "extreme" case in which one unhappy bridedaughter organized a club for other bridedaughters in which members paid an entrance fee and lived together (1981, 258). He does not describe, however, any regular separate residence for girls or bridedaughters.

In Hui-an county, an agricultural area, delayed transfer marriage was organized differently with respect to labor. Bridedaughters were expected to contribute labor both to their natal family with whom they resided and, at harvesttimes, to their husband's family. (This pattern of harvesttime labor contributions for bridedaughters was also reported among the P'u-i, the non-Han group mentioned above; Chao and Chün 1981; Kung and Shih 1981; Mo 1981.) Unfortunately, we do not know if this labor pattern was long-established in Hui-an county, and therefore a distinctive historical development, or recently introduced. Perhaps in more outlying districts practicing delayed transfer marriage in the Canton Delta—from which I have as yet no informants—we would also find a different organization of labor. Certainly the development of the distinctive "four-water-six-land" system of sericulture itself needs further investigation. If sericulture is associated with delayed transfer marriage else-

*Lin provides statistics on the length of intervals of postmarital separation for one village in Hui-an county. Of 757 married women, 5 were separated from their husband for more than twenty years, 41 for more than ten years, 216 for more than six years, 351 for more than five years, and presumably the rest (144) for less than five years at the time of the survey (1981, 259). How should these relatively lengthy intervals be interpreted? Was the system of delayed transfer marriage in Fukien linked to labor as in the sericultural area in the Canton Delta? What was the effect of the tremendous political and economic upheavals—including civil war—on the marriage system in Hui-an, and specifically on the length of intervals of postmarital separation? Unfortunately, we do not have sufficient information to answer these important questions.

where in the Lingnan region, was it organized as in the four:six system described for the Canton Delta?

With respect to one feature of delayed transfer marriage, there are similarities between an outlying county in the Canton Delta—peripheral to the core delayed transfer marriage area—and Hui-an county in Fukien. In both Goumihng county in the Canton Delta and Hui-an county in Fukien, bridedaughters reportedly wore a face covering—a hat or veil—when visiting their husband's family. Perhaps where the pressures of sinicization were lighter, we will find that other non-Han traits persist in association with the practice of delayed transfer marriage—or that typically Chinese cultural traits are absent in those areas practicing delayed transfer marriage. This is also suggested by Lin's report that Fukien villages practicing delayed transfer marriage seldom practiced footbinding, a distinctively Chinese cultural trait. By contrast, my own data from the core of the delayed transfer area in the Canton Delta do not show a strong association between marriage and unbound feet. Many other correlations between the practice of delayed transfer marriage and specific cultural traits need to be explored, both within and across the two delayed transfer areas and local ethnic groups.*

*Among the many cultural features that may be found in association with delayed transfer marriage beyond the Canton Delta is the festival celebrating the myth of the cowherd and the weaving maiden and her sisters. Was the Seven Sisters festival an important occasion for girls in Hui-an county in Fukien? Did this festival occupy a central place in the annual ritual cycle among ethnic groups of the Lingnan region who practiced delayed transfer? These are questions for future research. Eberhard, who pioneered research on the ethnic associations of elements of Chinese culture, may provide a key in a work that has only recently come to my attention. According to Eberhard, various features of the myth underlying the Seven Sisters festival can be attributed to Chuang culture (1941, 60–62).

One practice found within the Chinese cultural repertoire that may be absent from delayed transfer areas is female infanticide. Did the practice of female infanticide vary by region and was it found in the delayed transfer area of the Canton Delta? Given a daughter's relatively greater labor value in the delayed transfer area in the Delta, we might expect a low incidence of female infanticide there. Although data on the distribution of the practice of female infanticide in China are sparse, the accounts of some observers seem to indicate that the practice did vary by region (Abel 1818; Williams 1849; Gray 1875; Giles 1914). Two longtime residents of Canton, John Henry Gray (1875) and George T. Lay (1841), reported that female infanticide was not prevalent in that area. S. Wells Williams

The ethnic associations of the delayed transfer marriage systems in both Kwangtung and Fukien thus raise interesting questions concerning the origin of regional variation in Chinese marriage customs and culture. Answers to these questions must now await further research.

(1849) also notes reports of a low incidence in the Canton area. In my own field research, informants from the delayed transfer area who were questioned about this unanimously reported that female infanticide had not been practiced in their village. In addition, to the best of my knowledge, female infanticide was not practiced among the local ethnic groups in which delayed transfer marriage was found. Like footbinding, female infanticide appears to have been outside the cultural repertoire of those groups, and perhaps also of the Chinese in the delayed transfer area in the Canton Delta.

POSTSCRIPT

Postscript:
A Male Perspective
on Marriage

In a special interview session arranged in 1986 by James Hayes, my research assistant and I had the opportunity to talk with four Sundak men about delayed transfer marriage. This session was organized to elicit from a few men an account of delayed transfer marriage and the radical marriage alternatives. What did husbands think about the customary separation of husbands and wives? What did fathers think about compensating bride-daughters and sworn spinsters?

The four session participants, members of a Hong Kong association for people whose native place is Sundak county, came prepared to discuss delayed transfer marriage. Two informants were formally interviewed, and the other two contributed to the discussion. In this postscript, I provide an account of the first interview. Not only did the first informant prove exceptionally articulate in his description of delayed transfer marriage, he had also been selected by the other participants as their spokesman.

The informant was 74 years old, from Yuhng Keih, the large

silk center in Sundak. Delayed transfer marriage was the form of marriage practiced in Yuhng Keih, and the informant had married according to that practice. The informant said at the outset that he was prepared to give a full and accurate account of delayed transfer marriage because he knew both that I was writing a book and that this practice could be misinterpreted. I was interested to hear from the informant why he thought the delayed transfer form of marriage had arisen in Sundak. Clearly anticipating this question, the informant responded that there were several reasons, the first being economic. He said that traditionally Sundak women had had jobs. They could afford to be independent and support their natal family. In addition, a resident daughter-in-law was expected to serve her mother-in-law, doing many household chores, serving tea, and burning incense before the family's ancestors. Naturally, the informant observed, women didn't like those kinds of obligations. Before settling in the husband's home, women had few restrictions placed on them. Still another reason for the separation of spouses was that marriages in those days were blind, arranged matches. There was a distance between husbands and wives at marriage, one that the initial separation of spouses and regular conjugal visits helped overcome. A final reason given by the informant for the practice of delayed transfer marriage—a rationalization particularly informed by contemporary thought—was that although husbands traditionally had the authority in the family, wives in Sundak were able to stand up to them.

The informant described the postmarital separation of spouses in Yuhng Keih as lasting three years. During the first year of marriage, bridedaughters in Yuhng Keih visited the husband's family during New Year's and on other festival occasions. In the second and third years of marriage, according to the informant, bridedaughters visited anytime they liked, some choosing to visit more frequently. Husbands who were employed away from home returned for the visit of their spouses. The informant described the period of separation as marked by the ritual exchange of food between the families of the bridedaughter and her husband. During her visits, the bridedaughter took gifts of food to her husband's family. On festival occasions, the husband's family sent food to the bridedaughter's family, including prepared meats and special dumplings during the Dragonboat festival.

The informant's description of a bridedaughter's activities during visits in the husband's home matched the accounts given by my female informants. At the beginning of the cycle of visits, the bridedaughter did no chores in the husband's home, but as the time for her permanent settlement in his home approached, she gradually did more and more. When queried about obligations to serve tea and burn incense to the husband's ancestors, the informant explained that whether a woman had been married for only one year or many, it was her obligation to perform these duties every day she resided in her husband's home.

Since delayed transfer marriage was customary, didn't men in Yuhng Keih try and find wives who would settle with them immediately on marriage? No, very few men tried to find such a wife, the informant responded. Only women "with no status" (*mgau san fan*)—the muijai—immediately assumed residence with their husbands on marriage. The informant said that men didn't want muijai for wives; rather they preferred daughters from "normal families" (*potung yahn ga ge neuih*). Those daughters always waited a few years, usually three years, before settling in the husband's home. Clearly marriage to an immediately resident spouse would have been not altogether respectable in his eyes.

Had compensation marriage been practiced in Yuhng Keih? Yes, there had been this practice; even some of the informant's own female relatives had arranged compensation marriages. The informant explained that it was customary for a bride to return on the third day after marriage to her parents' home, where she stayed except on festival occasions. A bride who was not satisfied with her new husband—perhaps with the way he looked or with his family—might decide on returning to her home on the third day to arrange a compensation marriage. These brides themselves negotiated compensation, agreeing to pay the husband's family a sum of money, on the order of 400 dollars in silver. The husband's family then found another wife. The compensating bridedaughter consented to the second marriage and retained her authority as first wife. The husband and his compensating spouse remained husband and wife in name, and therefore the compensating bridedaughter could return to the husband's home to die, even though she had not met the obligations of a wife and daughter-in-law. Did mothers-in-law object to the arrangement of compensation marriages? The informant carefully considered his reply. Of course, mothers-in-law didn't like daughters-in-law to compensate, he conceded, but if they were determined to compensate, then there wasn't much a mother-in-law could do. How did husbands react to the payment of compensation? The informant hesitated, then replied that since the compensating bridedaughter gave the husband money to find a second wife, then it really didn't matter.

How popular was sworn spinsterhood in Yuhng Keih? "There were definitely more than just a few sworn spinsters in Yuhng Keih!" Of course, the majority of fathers didn't want their daughters to become sworn spinsters. Traditionally, Sundak fathers wanted their daughters to marry and have families of their own. It really depended on family circumstances, he added. If a father had daughters but no sons, and if the economic burden fell on the daughters, then he would certainly like one of his daughters to become a sworn spinster.

The formal interview ended with the questions on sworn spinsterhood. I had decided not to pursue the question of bride-initiated spirit marriage during this first interview with a male informant, because it dealt with the uncomfortable topic of death. The informant announced that although we had finished our questions, he had still more information on Sundak marriage practices to give us. To my surprise, he then proceeded to describe bride-initiated spirit marriage! He said that in Sundak there had been some girls who strongly opposed marriage. Since girls were not allowed to die at home, however, they had to find a place to die. These girls didn't want to have to die in some public place, so they had to find a husband's family to take their tablets. If there was a family with a deceased son of about the same age, then such a girl would try to arrange a spirit marriage for herself. Of course, as part of the arrangement, she agreed to care for her parents-in-law. Then, when she herself was sick or dying, she could move to her husband's home to die and have her tablet placed there. A girl arranged this kind of spirit marriage for herself, he said (*keuih jihgei ngon pai ge*).

The informant returned to the subject of the book I was writing, saying he wanted me to emphasize that the compensating bridedaughters, sworn spinsters, and wives of spirit husbands—all of whom he grouped together in one category—held a respected position in Sundak. Their conduct was praiseworthy, he said, because they took care of their parents and families, willingly sacrificing for their sake. Whatever they had, they contributed to their families. He gave as an illustration the case of his own domestic servant in Hong Kong, an elderly sworn spinster from Sundak. During the hard times in China in the early 1960's, this woman had spent half her yearly wages on food and supplies for her family back in Sundak. At that time, he said, it wasn't popular for Hong Kong people to return to their villages, but this kind of woman could still be seen visiting her family. The informant said, you could see just how well these women took care of their families. Why, of course, they didn't have to go—but they went, anyway.

APPENDIXES

The Right Question

How is it, I am frequently asked, that I was able to uncover a marriage system in a part of China that has long been the site of research, a region that has in fact the longest history of contact with the West? Or, as my editor asked after first reading my manuscript, How do we know you're not just making this up? In response, I usually first describe how misinterpretation (because of the cultural bias of outsiders) and political repression made this marriage system invisible. Then I relate how one informant during a key interview provided me with the essential bit of information that I needed to comprehend a system so different from "the" traditional Chinese marriage system. With this information, I was able to construct a question that elicited from informants a description of the organization and dynamics of the delayed transfer system.

My research project was to a great extent reshaped by the elderly women who were my informants and who preferred to talk about some things and not about others. The shift away from my initial focus on contemporary marriage and labor patterns in urban Hong Kong began with my first interviews. In the public setting of vegetarian halls and retirement homes, my questions about an informant's economic status seemed too personal and were rebuffed. I also quickly learned the constraints of conducting research in a colony. (Hong Kong was at the time of my research still under exclusively British administration.) Questions about an informant's economic strategies, savings, and investments became politically sensitive, even threatening, when asked by a researcher who was easily identified with the government. (This identification was reinforced by my dependence on official introductions for access to vegetarian halls and retirement homes to conduct my interviews.) But beyond these problems, my original research project was destined to fail because my informants found boring my questions about working conditions and employment histories in Hong Kong, and they could scarcely be persuaded to answer them. (I did not enjoy what I at least imagine to be the captive audience provided by a traditional village study!)

What the women did find enjoyable (and nonthreatening) was talking about their economic and marital strategies back in their natal villages in the Canton Delta. Gradually, therefore, my questions about women's lives in Hong Kong were replaced by ones about their earlier lives in the Delta (see pp. 5–8). Like most anthropologists doing research on China since the mid-1970's, I had read and been intrigued by Marjorie Topley's article on the forms of marriage resistance practiced by some women in the Canton Delta, and I began to ask questions suggested by Topley's analysis. Well into the first year of my research, one of my standard interview questions had become, Did women in your village practice marriage resistance and refuse to live with their husband (*mh lohk ga*)? For several months, answers to this question seemed to hold nothing unexpected. Most informants from sericultural villages responded affirmatively, and those from agricultural villages negatively, thus supporting a marriage-resistance interpretation. (That is, a woman employed in the silk industry had the economic means to live apart from her husband.) Then one day, an informant answered the question I asked but added something more, parenthetically, that was to prove a turning point in my research. She said that only a few women had refused to live with their husband—and that most women in her village had settled with their husband after three to four years of marriage. *Was* she saying that a wife regularly and customarily lived apart from her husband during the early years of marriage? For my assistant, Eunice Mei-wan Ku, and me, everything we thought we knew began at that moment to take on new meaning. With that interview, we learned to differentiate the radical practice of refusing to live with a husband from the norm of not immediately settling with him. In essence, we were able for the first time to lay aside our own culturally biased assumptions about how people in traditional Chinese society married and hear how some of them—several million of them in fact—did.

Marriage with delayed transfer was what informants had meant by "marriage," even though up until this point none had chosen to explain this. I attribute this mostly to a reticence on the part of informants to talk about a custom that they knew would seem strange in the eyes of foreigners and the younger generation in modern Hong Kong. (In fact, I did not meet a single person from that younger generation who knew about the delayed transfer marriages contracted by her grandparents.) In addition, for my elderly informants to volunteer information on delayed transfer marriage would have meant alluding to that early period of conjugal visits and the sexual behavior of bride-daughters, which was to prove a most delicate topic.

With our new understanding of marriage, my assistant and I were able to ask a new (and direct) question of our informants: In your village, did a bride settle with her husband immediately after marriage? Encouraged by the fact that other women from the delayed transfer area had obviously already told us everything, informants began to speak about that almost invisible form of marriage. On the basis of their accounts, we began to reconstruct the delayed transfer system as it had existed in the Canton Delta in the late nineteenth and early twentieth centuries.*

Looking back, although my informant's response that memorable day was unexpected, I was not unprepared to hear that marriage was organized differently in the Canton Delta, for I was of course familiar with Arthur Wolf's work on marriage variation in Fukien and Taiwan (see pp. 2–3). As a student of G. William Skinner's as well, I also knew that to explain the phenomenon of marriage with delayed transfer I had to determine, as well as I could, its distribution in time and space. Thus, as a consequence of that one interview, I changed not only the question I asked about marriage but my methodology as well, setting out to interview informants from villages across the Delta about marriage and labor patterns in their own and immediately ascending generations.

Anthropology has in recent years been characterized by a spirit of self-reflection that has brought a re-examination of the sources of anthropological knowledge. (See Geertz 1988; and Marcus and Fischer 1986.) How, for example, does the anthropologist know what she knows? My own research underscores the significance of the very construction of the questions anthropologists ask of their informants. What assumptions (and biases) underlie them and give them shape? It may not of course be possible to arrive at "right" questions—ones that are the most informed by the other culture—without experience in asking the wrong ones. Still, an awareness that our interpretation of other cultures rests as much on the questions we ask as on the answers we hear may prompt us to identify more quickly the biases that shape our questions.

---

*As the dynamics of the delayed transfer system became clear, I turned with mounting disbelief to the literature. Somewhere—in the gazetteers, missionary accounts, histories, travel literature—there had to be written confirmation of the oral accounts given me by my informants. That "confirmation" was first found in the history by John Henry Gray, which laid to rest the fear my assistant and I shared that somehow we had been mishearing our informants.

Character List

For place-names, see Appendix C. All terms and expressions are written according to the Yale system of Cantonese romanization, with the exception of a few terms for which Mandarin romanizations (M) are given.

baahk ching 白清

bik keuih sohei 迫佢梳起

bok 箔

chai-t'ang (M) 齋堂

che gung miuh 車公廟

chihsin 辭仙

ching yi giu 青衣轎

daaih huhng fa giu 大紅花轎

daaih ma 大媽

deih jyuh geuk　地 主 脚

di neuihjai hou jungyi kwahnmaaih yatchai
　　啲女仔好鐘意群埋一齊

dihng ching　訂 靖

dihng muhn hau　訂 門 口

dihng sahn jyu paaih　訂 神 主 牌

dong mui　當 妹

fongbihn so　方 便 所

ga sahnjyupaaih　嫁 神 主 牌

gansan　近 身

gatihngge gungjok　家 庭 嘅 工 作

gitfan　結 婚

go sahnjyupaaih ngon hai chitohng tuhngmaaih di jousin
　　yatchai　個神主牌安係祠堂同埋啲祖先一齊

gupoh nguk　姑 婆 屋

gwai ga gwai　鬼 嫁 鬼

gwo daaih laih　過 大 禮

gwo gei yu tohng　果 基 魚 塘

gwo mahn dihng　過 文 訂

hohk laih mauh　學 禮 貌

hoi nihn saang　開 年 生

hou bunsih　好 本 事

hou faai lohk ga　好 快 落 家

hou sai ji　好 細 緻

hou simahn　好 斯 文

jeui siu saam nihn sinji lohk ga　最 少 三 年 先 至 落 家

jih sihk keih lihk　自 食 其 力

jihgei wan ge　自己 搵 嘅

jihgei yuhnyi ge　自己 願意 嘅

jihso neuih　自梳 女

jikhaak lohk ga　即刻 落家

jikhaak puih chin　即刻 賠錢

jimui　姊妹

kai neuih　契女

keuih jihgei ngon paige　佢自己 安排 嘅

keuih nauyuhn la　佢嬲完嘥

kwahndeuih nguk　群隊 屋

laahk saan　勒山

leihsih　利是

loihloih wohngwohng　來來 往往

lohk ga　落家

maaih muhn hau　買 門 口

maaih mui　買 妹

mah nguk　嗎 屋

mai fu gaau　買 符 教

mauh　敲

mgao san fan　唔 夠 身 份

mh lohk ga　唔 落家

mouh ching　冒清

muhk tauh giu　木 頭 轎

muhk yu syu　木 魚 書

muhn hau　門 口

muijai　妹 仔

muijai nguk　妹 仔 屋

neuihjai nguk 女仔屋

potung yahn ga ge neuih 普通人家個女

pu lo-chia (M) 不落家

pu tso-chia (M) 不作家

puih chin wan go yih naai 賠錢搵個二奶

sai ma 細嬀

sau ching 守菁

sei tohng luhk deih 四堂六地

seung wan go jou 想搵個祖

sihng gai jai 承繼仔

sinleuhng miuh 仙娘廟

sohei 梳起

song gei yu tohng 桑基魚塘

touh dai 徒弟

tzu-shu nü (M) 自梳女

yahp fo 入伙

yatchai gwo muhn 一齊過門

yauh gaan nguk bei go sanneung 有間屋嘩個新娘

yauh mouh jikhaak lohk ga 有冇即刻落家

yauh san ga fan 有身家分

yiu wan wuhn hau 要搵門口

Place-names by County

Each place-name is followed by the number of informants (and/ or other sources) reporting for that place. The total number of informants for each county is listed after the county name. County seats are indicated with an asterisk. Because of space considerations, not all informants' villages (or counties) are shown on the maps.

Punyu (27) 番禺

pa   Louh Nga Gong Naahm Pin (1)   老鴉岡南片

pb   Sya Hoh Cheuhng Beng (1)   沙河長湴

pc   Loh Gong (1)   蘿岡

pd   Fo Chyun (1)   火村

pe   Siu Bak (1)   少北

pf   Hoh Naahm (1)   河南

pg San Jau Heui (1) 新州墟

ph Gun Saan Bui Gong (1) 官山貝岡

pi Jung Chyun (1) 種村

pj Daaih Luhng (1) 大龍

pk Lihn Fa (1) 蓮花

pl Sih Kiuh* (2) 市橋

pm Sya Waan (1) 沙灣

pn Wohng Gok (1) 黄角
    [map indicates Jungsaan]

po village outside Wohng Bou (1) 黄埔

pp Fa Deih Chah Gau (1) 花地茶滘

pq Daaih Sehk (1) 大石

pr Leih Yahn Dung Naahm Chyun (1) 里人洞南村

ps San Kiuh (1) 新橋

pt Seuhng Gauh (1) 上滘

Sundak (50) 順德

sa Bik Gong (2) 碧江

sb Chahn Chyun (old & new) (4) 陳村

sc Sin Chung (1) 仙涌

sd Mah Chyun (1) 馬村

se Hoh Chyun (1) 荷村

sf Lohk Chuhng (1) 樂從

sg Sya Gau (1) 沙均

sh Seui Tuhng (1) 水籐

si Lahk Lauh (3) 勒流（勒樓

sj Luhng Gong (1) 龍江

sk   Luhng Saan (2)   龍山

sl   Gam Juk Yauh Taan (1)   甘竹右灘

sm   Mahk Chyun (1)   麥村

sn   Gong Meih Ching Chah (1)   冈尾清茶

so   Gong Meih Laahm Bou (1)   冈尾藍保

sp   Gong Meih Gwon Ngon Heui (3)   冈尾均安墟

sq   Daaih Leuhng* & Bak Muhn (5)   大良, 北門

sr   Mah Gong (1)   馬冈

ss   Gwai Jau & Ngoih Chyun (5)   桂州, 外村

st   Yuhng Keih (5)   容奇

su   Bak Gau (1)   北滘

sv   Dung Mah Lihng (1)   東馬寧

sw   Chung Hohk (1)   冲鶴

Jungsaan (13)   中山

ja   Taahm Jau Heui (1)   燂州墟

jb   Siu Laahm & Waih Hau (5)   小欖, 圍

jc   Sehk Keih* (3)   石岐

jd   Hou Tauh (1)   壕頭

je   Saan Tohng Heung (1)   山塘鄉

jf   Wohng Bou (1)   黄圃

jg   Hoi Jau (1)   海洲

Naahmhoi (28)   南海

na   Lahm Ngohk (1)   林岳

nb   Pihng Jau (1)   平州

nc   Hah Paak (1)   下柏

nd Loh Haahng Heui (1) 蘿 行 墟

ne Sai Tiuh Daaih Sya (1) 西 樵 大 沙

nf Sai Tiuh Taai Pihng Heui (1) 西 樵 太 平 墟

ng Sai Tiuh Gaan Chyun (1) 西 樵 簡 村

nh Sai Tiuh Gun Saan (3) 西 樵 官 山

ni Sai Tiuh Hah Heui (1) 西 樵 下 墟

nj Gau Gong (2) 九 江

nk Faht Saan* (1) 佛 山

nl village between nd & ab (2)

nm Gam Jiu (1) 甘 蕉

nn Daaih Lihk Heui (1) 大 力 墟

no Pihng Deih Chyun (1) 平 地 村

np Sya Tauh (1) 沙 頭

nq Seuhng Paak (1) 上 柏

nr Gun Yiu Heui (1) 官 窰 墟

ns Yihm Bou Sihng (1) 鹽 步 城

nt Dihp Gau Heung (1) 疊 滘 鄉

nu Wong Gong (1) 橫 江

nv Seuhng Sai (1) 上 西

Hoksaan (2) 鶴 山

ha Gu Lu (1) 古 勞

hb Sya Pihng Heui (1) 沙 平 墟

Saamseui (7) 三 水

aa Baak Neih (1) 白 泥

ab Sai Naahm (2) 西 南

ac   Chek Gong Tauh Sai Chyun (1)   赤江頭西村
ad   Louh Bau Heui Jye Gaai (1)   芦包墟

Goumihng (2)   高明
ga   Gou Mihng* (1)   高明
gb   Seh Tohng Chyun (1)   虵塘村

Dunggun (7)   東莞
da   Sya Chyun (1)   沙村

Sanwui (6)   新會
wa   Gong Muhn (1)   江門
wb   San Wui* (1)   新會
wc   Dung Gaap San Tihn (1)   東甲新田

Seiwui (1)   四會
ea   Fung Lohk Waih (1)   豐樂圍
[map indicates Gouyiu co.]

Fayuhn (1)   花縣
fa   Lihn Fa Tohng (1)   蓮花塘

Toisaan (4)   台山
ta   San Cheuhng Heui (1)   新昌墟

Kwangtung Gazetteers Consulted

The Customs section of all gazetteers listed below has been surveyed; an asterisk indicates that the Biography section has also been surveyed.

Chan-chiang shih, 1972　湛江市誌

Ch'ang-le, 1845　長樂縣志

Ch'ao-yang, 1884　潮陽縣志

Ch'eng-hai, 1764, 1815　澄海縣志

Chia-ying chou, 1898　嘉應州志

Chieh-yang, 1890　揭陽縣續志

Ch'ih-ch'i, 1926　赤溪縣志

Ch'ing-yüan, 1880　靖遠縣志

Chiung-tung, 1820　瓊東縣志

Ch'iung-shan, 1857　瓊山縣志

Ch'ü-chiang, 1687, 1875 曲江縣志

En-p'ing, 1825, 1934 恩平縣志

Feng-ch'uan, 1835 封川縣志

Feng-shun, 1884 豐順縣志

Fo-kang, 1851 佛岡縣志

Hai-feng, 1750 海豐縣志

Hai-k'ang, 1687 海康縣志

Hai-yang, 1900 海陽縣志

Ho-p'ing, 1819 和平縣志

Hsi-ning, 1830 西寧縣志

*Hsiang-shan, 1750, 1827, 1863, 1873 香山縣志

Hsin-an, 1820 新安縣志

Hsin-hsing, 1758 新興縣志

*Hsin-hui, 1609, 1841 新會縣志

Hsin-ning, 1839, 1893 新寧縣志

Hsing-ning, 1811 興寧縣志

Hsü-wen, 1936 徐聞縣志

*Hua, 1687 花縣志

Hui-lai, 1731 惠來縣志

Jen-hua, 1883 仁化縣志

Kai-p'ing, 1823, 1933 開平縣志

Kan-en, 1931 感恩縣志

Kao-ming, 1894 高明縣志

Kao-yao, 1826, 1854 高要縣志

Kuang-ning, 1714 廣寧縣志

Kui-shan, 1783 歸善縣志

Lin-kao, 1892 臨高縣志

Lo-ch'ang, 1871, 1931　樂昌縣志

Lo-ting, 1935　羅定縣志

Lu-feng, 1745　陸豐縣志

Lung-ch'uan, 1818　龍川縣志

Lung-men, 1936　龍門縣志

Macau, 1751　澳門記略

Mao-ming, 1888　茂名縣志

Nan-ao, 1783　南澳縣志

Nan-hai, 1809, 1835, *1872, *1910　南海縣志

Nan-hai Fo-shan, 1752, 1830　南海佛山鎮志

Nan-hai Chiu-chiang, 1883　南海九江鄉志

P'an-yü, 1774, *1871, *1931　番禺縣志

P'ing-yüan, 1820　平遠縣志

P'u-ning, 1745　普寧縣志

San-shui, *1819, 1923　三水縣志

*Shih-ch'eng, 1931　石城縣志

Shih-hsing, 1926　始興縣志

*Shun-te, 1853, 1856, 1929　順德縣志

Shun-te Lung-chiang, 1926　順德龍江鄉志

Shun-te Lung-shan, 1805　順德龍山鄉志

Szu-hui, 1896　四會縣志

Sui-hsi, 1896　遂溪縣志

Ta-p'u, 1943　大埔縣志

Tan, 1934　儋縣志

Tien-pai, 1826　電白縣志

Ting-an, 1878　定安縣志

Tseng-ch'eng, 1820　增城縣志

Ts'ung-hua, 1710 從化縣志

*Tung-an, 1823 東安縣志

Tung-kuan, 1797, 1911, 1921 東莞縣志

Wen-ch'ang, 1858 文昌縣志

Weng-yüan, 1820 翁源縣志

Wu-ch'uan, 1824, 1892 吳川縣志

Yang-chiang, 1822 陽江縣志

Yang-ch'un, 1731 陽春縣志

Yang-shan, 1938 陽山縣志

Yung-an, 1822 永安縣志

REFERENCES CITED

References Cited

Abel, Clarke. 1818. *Narrative of a Journey in the Interior of China*. London: Longman, Hurst, Rees, Orme, and Brown.

Ahern, Emily M. 1973. *The Cult of the Dead in a Chinese Village*. Stanford, Calif.: Stanford University Press.

Ball, J. Dyer. 1901. *The Shun-tak Dialect*. Hong Kong: China Mail Office.

Benedict, Paul K. 1942. Thai, Kadai, and Indonesian. *American Anthropologist*, n.s. 44:576–601.

Bourdieu, Pierre. 1977. *Outline of a Theory of Practice*. Cambridge, Eng.: Cambridge University Press.

Burkhardt, V. R. 1953–58. *Chinese Creeds and Customs*. 3 vols. Hong Kong: South China Morning Post.

Chan, Anita; Richard Madsen; and Jonathan Unger. 1984. *Chen Village: The Recent History of a Peasant Community in Mao's China*. Berkeley: University of California Press.

Chao, Lin, and Ch'ing Chün. 1981. I-chung ch'i-t'e te ch'iang-hun hsing-shih (A special kind of capture marriage). *Hua-shih* (Fossil) 1: 15–16.

Chen, Han-seng. 1936. *Landlord and Peasant in South China*. New York: International Publishers.

Ch'en, Tung-yüan. 1933. *Chung-kuo fu-nü sheng-huo shih* (A history of women's life in China). Shanghai.

China, Imperial Maritime Customs. 1893. *Decennial Reports, 1882–1891.* Shanghai: Inspector General of Customs.

———. 1906. *Decennial Reports, 1892–1901.* Shanghai: Inspector General of Customs.

Chou Yüanhe. 1987. Chu-chiang san-chiao-chou te ch'eng-lu kuo-ch'eng (On the process of the formation of land in the Canton Delta). *Li-shih ti-li* (Historical Geography) 5:58–69.

Chung Kung-fu. 1958. Chu-chiang san-chiao-chou te sang-chi-yü-t'ang yü che-chi-yü-t'ang (Mulberry dike fish pond cultivation and sugarcane dike fish pond cultivation in the Canton Delta). *Ti-li hsüeh-pao (Acta Geographica Sinica)* 24, no. 3:257–72.

———. 1980. Chu-chiang san-chiao-chou te sang-chi-yü-t'ang (Mulberry dike fish pond cultivation on the Canton Delta: A complete artificial ecosystem of land-water interaction). *Ti-li hsüeh-pao (Acta Geographica Sinica)* 35, no. 3:200–209.

Dennys, Nicholas B. 1876. *The Folklore of China.* London: Trubner.

Eberhard, Wolfram. 1941. *Volksmärchen aus Südöst-China* (Folktales of southeast China). Helsinki: Suomalainen Tiedeakatemia Academia Scientiarum Fennica.

———. 1942. *Lokalkulturen im alten China*, Part 2, *Die Lokalkulturen des Südens und Ostens* (Local culture in traditional China, Part 2, The local culture of the south and the east). Peking: The Catholic University.

———. 1968. *The Local Cultures of South and East China* (Greatly abridged version of Eberhard 1942). Trans. Alide Eberhard. Leiden: E. J. Brill.

Eng, Robert Yeok-yin. 1978. *Imperialism and the Chinese Economy: The Canton and Shanghai Silk Industry, 1861–1932.* Ph.D. dissertation in History, University of California, Berkeley.

———. 1986. *Economic Imperialism in China: Silk Production and Exports, 1861–1932.* University of California, Berkeley, Institute of East Asian Studies, China Research Monograph 31. Berkeley: University of California Press.

Fabre, Alfred. 1935. Avril au pays des aïeux (April in the ancestral country). In *Catholic Church in China: Collectanea Commissionis Synodalis* 8:111–41.

Faure, David. 1986. *The Structure of Chinese Rural Society: Lineage and Village in the Eastern New Territories, Hong Kong.* Oxford: Oxford University Press.

Fong, H. D. 1934. China's Silk Reeling Industry: A Survey of Its Development and Distribution. *Monthly Bulletin on Economic China* 7, no. 12:483–506.

Fortune, Robert. 1857. *A Residence Among the Chinese.* London: John Murray.

Fo-shan ti-ch'ü ke-ming wei-yüan-hui (FSTC; Fo-shan District Revolutionary Committee). 1976. *Chu-chiang san-chiao-chou nung-yeh chih* (A study of the agriculture of the Canton Delta). 6 vols. Fo-shan.

Freedman, Maurice. 1958. *Lineage Organization in Southeastern China.* London: University of London, Athlone Press.

———. 1966. *Chinese Lineage and Society: Fukien and Kwangtung.* London: University of London, Athlone Press.

———. 1970. Ritual Aspects of Chinese Kinship and Marriage. In *Family and Kinship in Chinese Society,* ed. M. Freedman, pp. 164–87. Stanford, Calif.: Stanford University Press.

FSTC. *See* Fo-shan ti-ch'ü ke-ming wei-yüan-hui.

Geertz, Clifford. 1988. *Works and Lives: The Anthropologist as Author.* Stanford, Calif.: Stanford University Press.

Giles, Herbert A. 1914. *Adversaria Sinica.* Shanghai: Kelly & Walsh.

Gomes, Luís G. 1953. A festividade das sete irmas (The Seven Sisters festival). In *Festividades chinesas* (Chinese festivals), ed. Luís G. Gomes, pp. 215–21. Macau.

Gray, John Henry. 1875. *Walks in the City of Canton.* Hong Kong: De Souza.

———. 1878. *China: A History of the Laws, Manners and Customs of the People.* 2 vols. London: Macmillan.

Gray, Mrs. [John Henry]. 1880. *Fourteen Months in Canton.* London: Macmillan.

Greenway, Alice. 1987. Ah Bing and Her "Sisters." *Wilson Quarterly,* Summer: 152–61.

Hedde, Isidore. 1848. *Description méthodique des produits divers recueillis dans un voyage en chine* (A systematic description of various products collected on a voyage in China). Saint-Etienne: Imprimerie de Theolier Aine.

Henry, B. C. 1886. *Ling Nam or Interior Views of Southern China.* London: S. W. Partridge.

Ho, It Chong. 1958. *The Cantonese Domestic Amah: A Study of a Small Occupational Group of Chinese Women.* Research report, University of Malaya (Singapore).

Howard, C. W. 1923. *The Sericulture Industry of South China.* Canton: Canton Christian College, College of Agriculture.

Howard, C. W., and K. P. Buswell. 1925. *A Survey of the Silk Industry of South China.* Ling Nan Agricultural College, Canton Christian College, Department of Sericulture, Agricultural Bulletin no. 12. Hong Kong: Commercial Press.

Hsiang-shan hsien-chih (Gazetteer of Jungsaan county). 1827.

Hsiao, Kung-chuan. 1960. *Rural China.* Seattle: University of Washington Press.

Hsieh, Winston. N.d. *Silk and Guns in Modern China: Commercialization and Its Impact in the Canton Delta Region.* Unpublished manuscript.

Hu, P'u-an. 1935. Kwangsi. *Chung-hua ch'üan-kuo feng-su chih* (Gazetteer of Chinese customs). Part 1, vol. 9, 24–27.

————. 1936. Kwangtung. *Chung-hua ch'üan-kuo feng-su chih* (Gazetteer of Chinese customs). Part 2, vol. 7, 1–58.

Huang, Parker Po-fei. 1970. *Cantonese Dictionary.* New Haven, Conn.: Yale University Press.

Jaschok, Maria H. A. 1984. On the lives of women unwed by choice in pre-Communist China: Research in progress. *Republican China* 10, no. 1a:42–55.

————. 1987. Pattern and Choice: Alternatives to Orthodox Marriage in Pre-Communist China. In *Proceedings of the 8th International Symposium in Asian Studies,* pp. 263–83. Hong Kong: Asian Research Service.

K'ai, Shih. 1926. Kuang-tung-ti "pu-luo fu-chia" he "tzu-shu" (Kwangtung's *mh lohk ga* and *jihso*). *Hsin nü-hsing* (New woman) 1, no. 12: 937–42.

K'ao Huo. 1925. *Nan Chung-kuo ssu-yeh tiao-ch'a pao-kao-shu* (Report of the silk industry of South China). Canton: Ling-nan College Press.

Kung, P'ei-hua, and Shih Chi-chung. 1981. P'u-i-tzu hun-yin shih-hsi (A preliminary study of the marriage customs of the P'u-i people). *Kuei-chou min-tzu yen-chiu* 3:46–51.

Lay, George T. 1841. *The Chinese as They Are.* London: William Ball.

Lebar, Frank M., Gerald C. Hickey, and John K. Musgrave. 1964. *Ethnic Groups of Mainland Southeast Asia.* New Haven, Conn.: Human Relations Area Files Press.

Lei, Yue-wai, and Lei Hei-kit. 1925. Report on a Steam Filature in Kwangtung. *Lingnam Agricultural Review* 3:109–50.

Li, Kolu. 1927. *Die Seidenindustrie in China* (The silk industry of China). Ph.D. dissertation in Economics, Friedrich-Wilhelms Universität, Berlin.

Li, Lillian M. 1981. *China's Silk Trade.* Cambridge, Mass.: Harvard University Press.

Liang, Shao-jen. 1837. *Liang-pan ch'iu-yü an sui-pi* (Miscellaneous notes from the studio called "Two Kinds of Autumn Rain"). Shanghai: Sao-yeh shan-fang.

Liao, Ch'ung-chen. 1934. Kuang-tung fu-nü-chieh tui-yü ts'an-su fu-hsing yün-tung ying yu chih kung-hsien (The contribution of Kwangtung women to the worm and silk industry). In *Shun-te hsien ts'an-su chan-lan-hui, ti-i-ts'u* (The first worm and silk exhibition of Sundak county), pp. 1–6.

Lin, Hui-hsiang. 1981. Lun ch'ang-chu-niang-chia feng-su te ch'i-yüan chi mu-hsi-chih tao fu-hsi-chih te kuo-tu (A discussion of the origins of the long-term residence of wives in the natal home and the transition from matriarchy to patriarchy). In *Lin Hui-hsiang jen-lei-hsüeh lun chu* (Lin Hui-hsiang's works on anthropology), pp. 254–88. Fukien.

Liu Po-yüan. 1922. *Kuang-tung ssu-yeh tiao-ch'a pao-kao-shu* (Report of the silk industry of Kwangtung province). Canton: Experimental Farm of Kwangtung.

Lo, Dorothy, and Leon Comber. 1958. *Chinese Festivals in Malaya.* Singapore: Eastern Universities Press.

Mann, Susan. 1987. Women and Work in the Qing Period. Paper presented at the Symposium on Women in Traditional and Contemporary China, Center for Chinese Studies, University of California, Berkeley, 2 May 1987.

Marcus, G., and M. Fischer. 1986. *Anthropology as Cultural Critique: An Experimental Moment in the Human Sciences.* Chicago: University of Chicago Press.

Miao Hung-chi and Ch'en Hua-ts'ai. 1966. Nung-yeh t'u-ti lei-hsing te yen-chiu yü chih-t'u: I Chu-chiang san-chiao-chou Chung-shan P'an-yü hsien wei li (A study of the types of agricultural terrain and their mapping: The case of Jungsaan and Punyu counties in the Canton Delta). *Ti-li hsüeh-pao (Acta Geographica Sinica)* 32, no. 1: 74–81.

Mo, Chun-ch'ing. 1981. Pien-tan shan P'u-i-tzu te "tai-chia-ke" feng-su (The *tai-chia-ke* custom of the P'u-i people of Pien-tan shan). *Kuei-chou min-tzu yen-chiu* 1:63–69.

Moser, Leo J. 1985. *The Chinese Mosaic: The Peoples and Provinces of China.* Boulder, Colo.: Westview Press.

Nan-hai hsien-chih (Gazetteer of Naahmhoi county). 1910.

P'an-yü hsien-chih (Gazetteer of Punyu county). 1871.

Parish, William L., and Martin King Whyte. 1978. *Village and Family in Contemporary China.* Chicago: University of Chicago Press.

Peplow, S. H., and M. Barker. 1931. *Hongkong, Around and About.* 2d ed. Hong Kong: Ye Olde Printerie.

Potter, Jack M. 1970. Land and Lineage in Traditional China. In *Family and Kinship in Chinese Society,* ed. Maurice Freedman, pp. 121–38. Stanford, Calif.: Stanford University Press.

Pulleyblank, E. G. 1983. The Chinese and Their Neighbors in Prehistoric and Early Historic Times. In *The Origins of Chinese Civilization,* ed. David N. Keightly, pp. 411–66. Berkeley: University of California Press.

Ross, Edward Alsworth. 1911. *The Changing Chinese.* New York: Century.

Sampson, Theos. 1868. Anti-marriage Associations. *Notes and Queries on China and Japan* 9:142–43.

Sankar, Andrea P. 1978. *The Evolution of the Sisterhood in Traditional Chi-*

nese Society: From Village Girls' Houses to Chai T'angs in Hong Kong.
Ph.D. dissertation in Anthropology, University of Michigan.

———. 1984. Spinster Sisterhoods. In *Lives: Chinese Working Women*, ed.
Mary Sheridan and Janet W. Salaff, pp. 51–70. Bloomington: In-
diana University Press.

———. 1985. Sisters and Brothers, Lovers and Enemies: Marriage Resistance in Southern Kwangtung. *Journal of Homosexuality* 11, no.
3/4:69–81.

Scherzer, Karl von, ed. 1872. *Fachmännische Berichte über die öster-
reichisch-ungarische Expedition nach Siam, China und Japan* (A technical
report on the Austrian-Hungarian expedition to Siam, China and
Japan). Stuttgart: Julius Maier.

Semmedo, Alvaro (Alvarez). 1655. *The History of That Great and Renowned Monarchy of China*. Trans. from the Italian. London: E. Tyler.

Shih, Min-hsiung. 1976. *The Silk Industry in Ch'ing China*. Trans. by E-tu
Zen Sun. Ann Arbor: University of Michigan, Center for Chinese
Studies.

Shirokogoroff, Sergei M. 1931. New Contribution to the Problem of the
Origin of Chinese Culture. *Anthropos* 26:217–22.

Shun-te feng-mao (A look at Sundak county). 1985. Sundak: Hsiang-ch'in
Ta-hsüeh, Shun-te Hsia-yu Hui, Pien-hsieh-tsu.

Shun-te hsien-chih (Gazetteer of Sundak county). 1853.

Shun-te hsien-chih (Gazetteer of Sundak county). 1856.

Ssu-t'u Shang-chi. 1986. Ming-tai Kuang-tung ching-chi ti-li ch'u-t'an
(A tentative inquiry into the economic geography of Kwangtung in
the Ming dynasty). *Li-shih ti-li* (Historical Geography) 4:102–18.

Skinner, G. William. 1977. Regional Urbanization in Nineteenth-
Century China. In *The City in Late Imperial China*, ed. G. William
Skinner, pp. 211–49. Stanford, Calif.: Stanford University Press.

Smedley, Agnes. 1943. *Battle Hymn of China*. New York: Knopf.

Smith, Arthur H. 1899. *Village Life in China*. New York: Revell.

So, Alvin Yiu-cheong. 1982. *Gentry and the Capitalist World-System: A
Study of the Political Economy of the South China Silk District*. Ph.D. dissertation in Sociology, University of California, Los Angeles.

———. 1986. *The South China Silk District: Local Historical Transformation
and World-System Theory*. Albany: SUNY Press.

Spencer, Robert F., and S. A. Barrett. 1948. Notes on a Bachelor House
in the South China Area. *American Anthropologist* 50:463–78.

Stübel, Hans. 1976. *Die Li Stämme der Insel Hainan* (The Li peoples of
Hainan). Asian Folklore and Social Life Monographs, ed. Lou Tsu-
k'uang, vols. 83–84. Taipei: Orient Cultural Service.

Thomson, John Stuart. 1909. *The Chinese*. Indianapolis: Bobbs-Merrill.

Tien, Tsung. 1952. Women Who Do Not Marry. *The Orient*, July: 41–43.

Topley, Marjorie. 1958. *The Organization and Social Function of Women's Chai T'ang in Singapore*. Ph.D. dissertation, University of London.

———. 1973. "Women's Liberation" in Traditional China: The Anti-marriage Movement of Kwangtung. Paper prepared for the Canton Delta Seminar, Centre of Asian Studies, University of Hong Kong.

———. 1975. Marriage Resistance in Rural Kwangtung. In *Women in Chinese Society*, ed. Margery Wolf and Roxane Witke, pp. 67–88. Stanford, Calif.: Stanford University Press.

Trewartha, Glenn T. 1939. Field Observation on the Canton Delta of South China. *Economic Geography* 15:1–11.

Tsao, Sung-yeh. 1929. Kuan-yü pu lo-chia (Concerning the custom of *pu lo-chia*). *Min-tzu* 74:20–21.

Wiens, Herold J. 1967. *Han Chinese Expansion in South China*. Hamden, Conn.: Shoe String Press.

Williams, S. Wells. 1849. *The Middle Kingdom*. 3d ed. New York: John Wiley.

Wolf, Arthur P. 1974, Gods, Ghosts, and Ancestors. In *Religion and Ritual in Chinese Society*, ed. A. P. Wolf, pp. 131–82. Stanford, Calif.: Stanford University Press.

Wolf, Arthur P., and Chieh-shan Huang. 1980. *Marriage and Adoption in China, 1845–1945*. Stanford, Calif.: Stanford University Press.

Wolf, Margery. 1972. *Women and the Family in Rural Taiwan*. Stanford, Calif.: Stanford University Press.

———. 1975. Women and Suicide in China. In *Women in Chinese Society*, ed. Margery Wolf and Roxane Witke, pp. 111–41. Stanford, Calif.: Stanford University Press.

Wong, C. S. 1967. *A Cycle of Chinese Festivities*. Singapore: Malaysia Publishing House.

Yang, Martin C. 1945. *A Chinese Village: Taitou, Shantung Province*. New York: Columbia University Press.

INDEX

Index

In this index an "f" after a number indicates a separate reference on the next page, and an "ff" indicates separate references on the next two pages. A continuous discussion over two or more pages is indicated by a span of page numbers, e.g., "57–59." *Passim* is used for a cluster of references in close but not consecutive sequence.

dence, 98–100; organization, 98–100; spatial distribution, 164. *See also* Spirit marriage
Bridewealth, 29, 52, 57, 98, 124
Buswell, K. P., 135n, 141, 147, 154, 156, 161

Ch'en, Ch'i-yüan, 146–47
Chen, Han-seng, 141, 158
Compensation marriage, 8, 18, 30, 92, 97, 100, 179; and sericulture, 39, 52–54, 126, 133–34, 159–60, 163, 168; description, 48, 51, 68, 181–82; funds for, 48–49, 52, 59, 69, 181; purpose, 49–50, 68; constraints on practice, 50–51, 60–61, 64, 69; spatial distribution, 51, 163–64; temporal distribution, 51, 53–54, 63, 65, 117–18, 127–29, 132–34, 160, 164, 168–69; distinguished from delayed transfer marriage, 52, 111f, 168; arrangements, 58–62, 67, 69; early compensation, 66–67, 163; late compensation, 66–67, 163; children in, 68–69; origins, 122–26, 132, 168
Conjugal visits, *see under* Bridedaughters

Delayed transfer marriage: description, 3–5, 12, 108–12, 180–81; intervals of spousal separation, 4–5, 25–27, 29, 61, 64, 105, 107, 112–17 *passim*, 158, 167–68, 173n; and sericulture, 7–8, 14, 135–36, 140, 147, 148–60 *passim*, 167–68; spatial distribution, 8–9, 10–11, 102–3, 105, 135f, 162; core area, 9, 102, 174; consummation of, 18f, 48, 65, 68; age at marriage, 29; women's community, 32, 45–47; political repression of, 41, 102, 105, 107–8, 112–16, 122; cultural bias toward, 41, 102, 106–7, 116; distinguished from compensation marriage, 52, 111f, 168; arrangement of, 55–58; marriage-

resistance portrayals of, 105–7, 110–11, 116, 123; contemporary status, 113, 115–16; origins, 167, 171. *See also* Bridedaughters; Wives
Domestic service, 52, 71, 73, 78f, 128, 164, 169, 183
Double Seven festival, 41–42. *See also* Seven Sisters festival
Dowry, 21, 29, 52, 57f, 67
Dunggun county, 8, 33, 35, 125

Eberhard, Wolfram, 113n, 170n, 171n, 174
Ethnic groups: Chuang, 170f; Li, 170, 171n; P'u-i, 170f, 173

Fabre, Alfred, 16–17n, 93n
Father's sisters, *see* Paternal aunts
Faure, David, 37n
Female infanticide, 174–75n
Feng, Ju-t'ang, 108–9, 118, 124
Festivals, 12f, 17n, 181; Ch'ing Ming, 12f, 16–17n. *See also* Bridedaughters; Seven Sisters festival
Footbinding, 54, 175n
Fortune, Robert, 144
Friendship, female, 45. *See also* Girls' houses; Seven Sisters festival
Fukien province, 190; minor marriage, 2–3; delayed transfer marriage, 113–15, 172–74

Gansan (personal maid), 20, 29, 132
Gazetteers: Sundak county, 9n, 23, 106, 108n, 109, 118, 123n; description, 105; Punyu county, 106n, 119, 123n, 172; Jungsaan [Hsiang-shan] county, 106n; Naahmhoi county, 108, 118, 124. *See also* Appendix D
"Ghost marries ghost," *see* Spirit marriage
Girls' houses, 6, 41, 120–21; description, 31, 34; organization, 32, 34–38, 45–47; recruitment, 33, 35–36, 40, 45ff; spatial distribution, 33–34, 171, 173; function,

Library of Congress Cataloging-in-Publication Data

Stockard, Janice E.
  Daughters of the Canton Delta : marriage patterns and economic
strategies in South China, 1860–1930 / Janice E. Stockard.
      p.   cm.
  Bibliography: p.
  Includes index.
  ISBN 0-8047-1392-8 (cl.): ISBN 0-8047-2014-2 (pbk.)
    1. Marriage—China—History—19th century.   2. Marriage—China—
History—20th century.   3. China—Social life and customs.
I. Title.
HQ684.A37 1989
306.8′1′0951—dc19   88-23551
                                                          CIP

This book is printed on acid-free paper.